AN APPLICATION GUIDE TO
TRANSFORMATIONAL EDUCATION

A Teacher's Handbook for Driving Student Success

AN APPLICATION GUIDE TO TRANSFORMATIONAL EDUCATION
Redefining Leadership in the Classroom

GT FREEMAN and APRIL THOMAS

FlutterBy Press

Copyright © 2025 by The Lincoln Center for Family and Youth

All rights reserved.
No part of this publication may be reproduced, stored
in a retrieval system, or transmitted in any form or by any means electronic,
mechanical, photocopying, recording or otherwise, without the prior written
permission of the publisher.

Published by
FlutterBy Press | www.flutterbypress.com

Publisher's Cataloging-in-Publication Data
Freeman, G.T.

An application guide to transformational education : redefining leadership in the classroom / G.T. Freeman and April Thomas. – Audubon, PA : FlutterBy Press, 2025.

p. ; cm.

ISBN13: 978-0-9601259-1-3

1. Educational leadership 2. School management and organization. 3. Educational innovations. I. Title. II. Freeman, G.T. III. Thomas, April.

LB2806 .F75 2024
371.2--dc23

Project Coordination
Jenkins Group, Inc. | www.jenkinsgroupinc.com

Design Credits
Cover design: Yvonne Fetig Roehler
Interior design: Brooke Camfield

Printing
Printed in the United States of America
29 28 27 26 25 • 5 4 3 2 1

Dedication

This workbook is dedicated to all the teachers who see their students not as empty vessels to be filled, but as fertile ground ready to be nurtured. To those who ignite curiosity rather than simply impart knowledge, who encourage exploration rather than conformity, and who foster the courage to question rather than the pressure to comply. You are the ones who water the deserts of the mind, bringing life, growth, and transformation where others see barrenness. Thank you for being the light that guides, the hand that lifts, and the heart that believes in the potential of every learner. You are the true cultivators of change in this world.

Contents

Acknowledgments	ix
About the Authors	x
About The Lincoln Center for Family and Youth	xi
Preface	xii
An Introduction to the Workbook	3

Chapter 1
Practicing Teacher Behaviors — 7

Section 1A	Self-Assessment and Reflection	8
Section 1B	Case Studies	16
Section 1C	Lesson Planning Activities	21
Section 1D	Reflection and Discussion	39
Section 1E	Peer Mentorship	41
Section 1F	Scenario	51
Section 1G	Role-Playing	55
Section 1H	Interdisciplinary and Collaborative Lesson Planning	62

Chapter 2
Cultivating School Climate — 75

Section 2A	Self-Assessment and Reflection	76
Section 2B	Case Studies	83
Section 2C	Lesson Planning Activities	88
Section 2D	Reflection and Discussion	96
Section 2E	Peer Mentorship	98
Section 2F	Scenarios	104
Section 2G	Role-Playing	108
Section 2H	Interdisciplinary and Collaborative Lesson Planning	118

CHAPTER 3
Promoting Student Wellness 123
    Section 3A   Self-Assessment and Reflection 124
    Section 3B   Case Studies 133
    Section 3C   Lesson Planning Activities 138
    Section 3D   Reflection and Discussion 150
    Section 3E   Peer Mentorship 153
    Section 3F   Scenarios 160
    Section 3G   Role-Playing 167
    Section 3H   Interdisciplinary and Collaborative Lesson Planning   177

CHAPTER 4
Improving Student Performance 189
    Section 4A   Self-Assessment and Reflection 190
    Section 4B   Case Studies 197
    Section 4C   Lesson Planning Activities 202
    Section 4D   Reflection and Discussion 213
    Section 4E   Peer Mentorship 216
    Section 4F   Scenarios 223
    Section 4G   Role-Playing 233
    Section 4H   Interdisciplinary and Collaborative Lesson Planning   240

Acknowledgments

For their leadership and support of The Lincoln Center (TLC), our sincerest gratitude is extended to TLC's Board of Directors: Scott Patrohay, Dr. Donna Sarhaan, Henrietta Heisler, Bob Holland, Dr. Latanya King, Joe Pailin, Dodie Williams, and Kirk Wycoff.

We also thank Dr. MaryJo Burchard and Jay Blackstone for their pivotal roles in codifying the Transformational Education model. To our TLC colleagues—Kerri Blakey, Rob D'Alonzo, Sara Dryka, Emily Gatto, Meghan Keaveny, Michael Quintiliano, and Michael Venzke—we are grateful for your passion for education, your commitment to serving the underserved, and for making each workday fulfilling and enjoyable.

Finally, we offer our deepest thanks to writer-editor Amy Lynch and educational consultant Kathryn Smink for their support, insight, and expertise. Their academic credentials and experience as educators proved invaluable in developing the self-assessments, case studies, and lesson-planning activities. This book would not have been possible without their assistance.

—GT Freeman and April Thomas

About the Authors

DR. GT FREEMAN is is the president and CEO of The Lincoln Center for Family and Youth, an entrepreneurial social enterprise providing education, coaching, and counseling. His diverse background in education includes roles as an adjunct professor, senior evaluator for US Department of Education grants, program director of executive education at a university, and headmaster of a private K–12 school. GT holds degrees in engineering, business administration, and organizational leadership.

APRIL THOMAS serves as the chief schools officer at TLC Leadership Academies, a network of alternative schools dedicated to educating and counseling nontraditional students. She holds Pennsylvania certifications in reading (K–12), english (7–12), and principalship (K–12) and has broad experience in teaching and leadership roles across private and public schools. April earned degrees in reading, english, and sociology and is currently pursuing a doctoral degree in educational leadership.

About The Lincoln Center for Family and Youth

The Lincoln Center (TLC), founded in 1970 by a behavioral health hospital and incorporated in 1983 as a 501(c)(3) nonprofit, is an entrepreneurial social enterprise dedicated to transforming lives and communities—one moment, one choice, one connection at a time. Headquartered in Philadelphia, TLC extends its reach across multiple states providing K-12 alternative education, comprehensive mental and behavioral health counseling, wellness coaching, and trauma-informed training. TLC also offers grant-writing support to assist school districts, universities, hospitals, police departments, and other nonprofit agencies in securing funding.

TLC is comprised of five programs: TLC Leadership Academies, TLC Education Institute, TLC Wellness, School-Based Services, and Community-Based Services. These programs unite under TLC's mission of "empowering people to make positive choices, meaningful connections, and transformational change."

For more information about The Lincoln Center for Family and Youth, please visit TheLincolnCenter.com

Preface

Welcome to *An Application Guide to Transformational Education: Redefining Leadership in the Classroom*. This guide serves as a practical, hands-on resource for applying the principles of Transformational Education (TE) in schools. Inside, you'll find a plethora of of tools—including lesson plans, case studies, and self-evaluation exercises—to help bring TE concepts to life in your classroom.

At the heart of the TE model is the belief that teachers are not just educators but pivotal leaders in shaping school culture and student success. The model highlights the powerful connection between teacher actions, school climate, student well-being, and academic achievement. To foster positive outcomes, TE identifies four essential teacher actions: building authentic relationships with students, helping learners find purpose in both their studies and their lives, providing personalized support, and cultivating a classroom environment rich in curiosity and exploration.

For a deeper understanding of the theoretical framework behind TE, we invite you to explore *An Introduction to Transformational Education: Redefining Leadership in the Classroom*. Grounded in scholarly research and the principles of Transformational Leadership, this foundational text presents a new approach to school leadership, urging teachers to lead through influence, inspiration, and meaningful support.

While the foundational book is intended for a broad audience of educators, administrators, parents, and lifelong learners interested in the transformative power of education, this companion workbook is specifically tailored for teachers. It offers practical strategies to help you integrate TE into your daily practice, empowering you to lead with purpose and make a lasting impact on your students.

An Application Guide to Transformational Education: Redefining Leadership in the Classroom

An Introduction to the Workbook

This workbook consists of four chapters, which are designed to accompany the same respective four chapters of the foundational book—*An Introduction to Transformational Education: Redefining Leadership in the Classroom*.

Chapter 1 pertains to the four TE teacher *behavior* variables: authentic engagement, meaning making, personalized support, and stimulating curiosity. Chapter 2 supports the three factors of *school climate*: support, kindness, and aesthetic guidance. Chapter 3 focus on the three dimensions of student wellness: connectedness, self-efficacy, and socio-emotional well-being. Finally, Chapter 4 focuses on three primary outcome measures: student engagement, academic performance, and prosocial behaviors. The relationships among these constructs are shown in Figure 1.

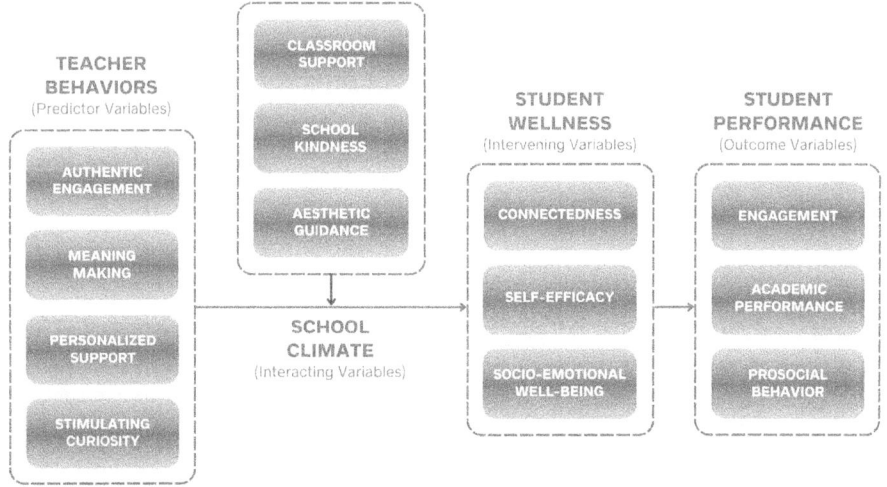

Figure 1: Relationships among variables in the Transformational Education model

Each chapter of the workbook contains eight sections: (a) Self-Assessment and Reflection, (b) Case Studies, (c) Lesson Planning Activities, (d) Reflection and Discussion, (e) Peer Mentorship, (f) Scenarios, (g) Role-Playing, and (h) Interdisciplinary and Collaborative Lesson Planning. Following is a brief description of each section.

Section A: The **Self-Assessment and Reflection** sections contains tools that allow educators to self-evaluate and reflect on their perceived effectiveness in implementing the TE model in their classroom.

Section B: The *Case Studies* sections present real or hypothetical scenarios that teachers may encounter in their classrooms. They're designed to illicit reflection as educators to analyze hypothetical situations, identify the challenges, and propose solutions based on the concepts of the TE model.

Section C: The *Lesson Planning Activities* sections, a lesson planning template as well as sample lesson plans are provided to engage students in authentic and meaningful learning experiences, catering to students with different learning styles and interests, while making the learning process intellectually stimulating.

Section D: The *Reflection and Discussion* sections promote collaboration and knowledge sharing among teachers. The activities in these sections provide opportunities for educators to discuss educational theories, their applications, and their implications for teaching and learning.

Section E: The *Peer Mentorship* sections contains forms that allow educators to collect information from a mentor or colleague using a 360-degree feedback form.

Section F: The *Scenarios* sections presents a specific teaching scenario and asks teachers to apply the theories and strategies they have learned to address the challenges or opportunities presented.

Section G: The *Role-Playing* sections provide opportunities for teachers to simulate instructional scenarios or interactions with students using role-playing exercises to assist them in exploring different teaching approaches, experimenting with strategies, and gaining insights into the practical applications of educational theories.

Section H: Finally, the *Interdisciplinary and Collaborative Lesson Planning* sections provides multiple examples of cross-curricular lesson plans, as well as a generic lesson plan template.

The first three sections (Section A–C) of each chapter focus on the *individual* teacher, providing self-reflection activities, as well as lesson planning templates and samples based on the principles of TE. The remaining five sections (Sections D–H) of each chapter focus on *groups* for the purpose of professional development, department collaboration, coaching, and mentoring.

Chapter 1

Practicing Teacher Behaviors

This chapter contains several exercises and applications to help teachers apply the theoretical content found in chapter 1 of the accompanying foundational text, *An Introduction to Transformational Education*. These exercises are designed to enhance understanding, promote critical thinking, and provide practical examples for educators. These various applications and exercises in educational theory textbooks aim to bridge the gap between theory and practice, allowing teachers to actively engage with the content and apply it to their teaching contexts.

- **Section 1A: Self-Assessment and Reflection**
- **Section 1B: Case Studies**
- **Section 1C: Lesson Planning Activities**
- **Section 1D: Reflection and Discussion**
- **Section 1E: Peer Mentorship**
- **Section 1F: Scenarios**
- **Section 1G: Role-Playing**
- **Section 1H: Interdisciplinary and Collaborative Lesson Planning**

Section 1A:
Self-Assessment and Reflection

The Teacher Behaviors Self-Assessment is a tool that allows educators to evaluate their teaching practices to help them reflect on their instructional practices, beliefs, and professional growth. **This self-assessment consists of four sections: Authentic Engagement, Meaning Making in the Classroom, Personalized Support, and Stimulating Curiosity.** It allows educators to critically examine their current practices and identify areas of strength and areas that may need improvement. Each section contains a series of statements related to the respective category.

Teacher Behavior Self-Assessment

Instructions: For each statement, indicate your agreement level or practice frequency.

5—Strongly Agree, 4—Agree, 3—Neutral, 2—Disagree, 1—Strongly Disagree

Authentic Engagement

Authentic engagement refers to creating a genuine connection between teachers and students, fostering a sense of community, and inspiring students' love for learning. Recognizing the importance of authentic engagement allows teachers to understand their role as leaders in shaping student outcomes. This self-assessment section helps teachers evaluate their commitment to fostering community, promoting intrinsic motivation, and serving as positive role models.

_____ 1. I believe that teachers have the power to positively affect students' lives over the long term.

_____ 2. I understand the importance of creating positive ripples of change through my teaching practices.

_____ 3. I recognize that my leadership as a teacher plays a significant role in determining outcomes for students and schools.

_____ 4. I strive to employ the behaviors advocated in Transformational Education to foster a sense of community and connection among students.

_____ 5. I believe that authentic engagement, meaning making, personalized support, and stimulating curiosity are crucial teacher behaviors in Transformational Education.

_____ 6. I understand that authentic engagement involves engaging students with internal controls, such as a love of learning and genuine interest in a subject.

_____ 7. I am committed to creating an intrinsically motivated learning environment where students value learning for its merits.

_____ 8. I believe in being an idealized influence for my students, demonstrating a commitment to and enthusiasm for learning goals.

_____ 9. I strive to be a positive role model for my students, gaining their admiration and trust through authenticity and dedication to education.

_____ 10. I encourage open communication and confidence in the learning process within my classroom community.

Authentic Engagement Total Score _____/50

Meaning Making

Meaning making involves guiding students to connect new knowledge and experiences with their existing understanding, promoting reflection, and encouraging prosocial values and behaviors. By actively inspiring and motivating students, setting clear learning goals, and nurturing a sense of purpose, teachers can enhance students' commitment to learning. This self-assessment section helps teachers gauge their effectiveness in creating meaningful learning experiences.

_____ 1. I actively inspire and motivate my students to rise above their ordinary experiences.

_____ 2. I consistently communicate clear learning goals that excite and engage my students.

_____ 3. I help students connect new knowledge and experiences to their previous knowledge.

_____ 4. I encourage students to reflect on the meaning and values conveyed by their choices.

_____ 5. I foster prosocial values and behaviors such as kindness, helping, and cooperation.

_____ 6. I create a sense of purpose in my students' lives by aligning their goals with their learning experiences.

_____ 7. I effectively lead and guide students to explore prosocial values through collaborative and helping behaviors.

_____ 8. I provide opportunities for students to be actively involved in the decision-making process in the classroom.

_____ 9. I promote a sense of community among my students, where they feel cared for and supported.

_____ 10. I consistently engage in behaviors that create meaning in my students' lives and enhance their commitment to learning.

Meaning Making Total Score _____/50

Personalized Support

Personalized support emphasizes building solid relationships with students, considering their needs and interests, and providing empathetic support. Teachers can create a supportive and inclusive classroom environment by tailoring instruction and actively listening to students. The personalized support section of the self-assessment enables educators to reflect on their efforts to meet the diverse needs of their students.

_____ 1. I prioritize building strong relationships with each of my students.

_____ 2. I consider each student's needs and interests when planning and delivering instruction.

_____ 3. I provide support and guidance to help students achieve their learning goals.

_____ 4. I am attentive to the unique talents and abilities of each student.

_____ 5. I actively listen to my students' concerns and provide empathetic support.

_____ 6. I encourage students to make decisions and actively participate in their learning.

_____ 7. I create a warm and supportive classroom environment.

_____ 8. I tailor my instruction to accommodate students with different backgrounds and abilities.

_____ 9. I take the time to develop a personal connection with each student.

_____ 10. I acknowledge and value the efforts and contributions of each student.

Personalized Support Total Score _____ /50

Stimulating Curiosity

Stimulating curiosity in the classroom encourages critical thinking, problem-solving, and creativity among students. Teachers can foster a culture of curiosity and intellectual growth by asking thought-provoking questions, embracing new ideas, and supporting independent thinking. The stimulating curiosity section of the self-assessment allows teachers to assess their ability to create an environment that nurtures curiosity and enhances students' cognitive and affective development.

_____ 1. I encourage students to think critically and reflect on the "how" and "why" of various topics.

_____ 2. I create opportunities for students to explore and solve problems that pique their curiosity.

_____ 3. I ask thought-provoking questions that stimulate students' intellectual curiosity.

_____ 4. I provide a supportive and nonjudgmental environment that encourages students to express their ideas and opinions freely.

_____ 5. I challenge assumptions and encourage students to think creatively and innovatively.

_____ 6. I welcome and embrace new ideas from students, fostering a culture of curiosity and exploration.

_____ 7. I support independent thinking among students, allowing them to develop their own solutions and approaches.

_____ 8. I recognize and affirm students' efforts in stimulating curiosity, creativity, and problem solving.

_____ 9. I actively seek to stimulate curiosity across different subjects and activities in the classroom.

_____ 10. I believe stimulating curiosity in the classroom increases students' affective and cognitive growth.

Stimulating Curiosity Total Score _____/50

Interpretation of Scores by Section:

Scoring:
- Add up your scores for all the statements.
- The higher the total score, the more you practice the target teacher behavior in the classroom.

Interpretation:
- 41–50: You effectively incorporate the target teacher behavior strategies in your classroom.
- 31–40: Your use of the target teacher behavior in the classroom is moderate. Continue to build on your current strategies to enhance this behavior.
- 21–30: You have some level of the target teacher behavior in your classroom, but there is room for improvement.
- 10–20: Your use of the target teacher behavior in the classroom may be limited.

Note: This self-assessment tool is designed to help you reflect on your current implementation of Transformational Education in the classroom or school setting. It is not a comprehensive evaluation but serves as a starting point for personal reflection and professional development.

Individual Reflection Questions
Transformational Education and Teacher Behaviors

This exercise aims to reinforce the significance of a teacher's role in shaping the lives of their students and promoting intrinsic motivation for lifelong learning. These thought-provoking questions prompt teachers to evaluate their effectiveness in creating positive classroom change. They can also help foster a supportive learning environment. Educators are encouraged to deeply reflect on their teaching practices and their impact on their students' growth and development.

Instructions: Utilize the following questions to reflect on your current teaching practices regarding the teacher behaviors discussed in chapter 1 of *An Introduction to Transformational Education*. You are encouraged to write your thoughts down for later reflection or discussion with a mentor.

1. Reflecting on your teaching practices, in what ways have you witnessed positive ripples of change being created? How do these experiences reinforce the importance of your role as a teacher?

2. Identify a specific example of how you have fostered a sense of community and connection among your students. How did this experience align with the behaviors advocated in Transformational Education?

3. How do you currently integrate the crucial teacher behaviors of authentic engagement, meaning making, personalized support, and stimulating curiosity in your classroom? In what ways do these behaviors contribute to creating an intrinsically motivated learning environment?

4. Reflect on your teaching practices and share how you inspire and motivate your students to go beyond their ordinary experiences. How does this approach contribute to their overall growth and academic achievement?

5. How do you ensure that you consistently communicate clear learning goals to your students in a way that excites and engages them? Share an experience where your students' understanding and enthusiasm were enhanced through this clear communication of goals.

6. Describe how you actively promote prosocial values and behaviors within your classroom, including kindness, helping, and cooperation. Share specific strategies you utilize to encourage these positive behaviors and cultivate a sense of community where students feel valued and supported. How do these intentional efforts enhance your students' overall learning experience?

7. Reflect on your teaching practices and describe how you prioritize building strong relationships with each of your students. Share a specific example of a student with whom you have established a strong connection and explain how this relationship has positively impacted their learning and overall development.

8. How do you provide support and guidance to help students achieve their learning goals? Share an experience where you offered practical support to a struggling student and explain how your assistance facilitated their progress and success.

9. Reflect on your approach to acknowledging and valuing the efforts and contributions of each student. Describe specific strategies you employ to ensure that every student feels recognized and appreciated in your classroom. Share an example of how this recognition has motivated students and positively influenced their self-esteem and participation in learning.

10. How do you employ thought-provoking questions to stimulate intellectual curiosity among your students? Can you share an example of a question that led to insightful discussions or a more profound exploration of a topic? How did this questioning approach contribute to your students' intellectual growth and development?

Section 1B: Case Studies

Case studies present real or hypothetical scenarios that teachers may encounter in their classrooms. They require educators to analyze the situation, identify challenges, and propose solutions based on the theories and concepts discussed in the textbook.

Instructions: Read the provided case studies carefully. Take note of the key points and important details presented in the text. Aim to arrive at well-rounded and thoughtful answers that consider various perspectives. Refer to the case study as needed to support your responses.

Mr. Fischer

In a bustling suburban neighborhood, Mr. Fischer, a dedicated English teacher, taught his ninth-grade English class with a fiery passion. His classroom became a stage as he transformed into different Shakespearean characters, captivating the students with his theatrical costumes and reciting famous monologues. Their curiosity awakened as they explored the timeless themes of love, tragedy, and power.

The students became immersed in the intricacies of the plays but struggled to understand the language and empathize with the characters. Mr. Fischer focused solely on dissecting the technical aspects of the text, neglecting the students' longing for deeper meaning.

Among them, Emily felt adrift in Shakespeare's complex language. She desired a connection to the characters and their struggles. Approaching Mr. Fischer, she shared her difficulty grasping the underlying themes and emotions. Mr. Fischer dismissed her concerns, prioritizing the technical understanding of the language.

Undeterred, Emily took matters into her own hands. She researched the historical context of the plays and watched modern adaptations. Through her exploration, she uncovered the relevance of Shakespeare's works in contemporary society, reigniting her curiosity. She yearned for Mr. Fischer to guide her on this journey of meaning making, but his focus remained solely on academic analysis.

Despite the absence of personalized support, Mr. Fischer's engaging teaching methods inspired the students. Lively class discussions and debates about Shakespearean characters' motivations became their delight. Curiosity flourished as they sought to unravel the complexities of the human condition depicted in the plays.

However, the lack of meaning making left a void in their understanding. They craved a deeper connection to the material, a sense of personal relevance that could breathe life into the ancient texts.

As the school year ended, the students reflected on their time in Mr. Fischer's class. They acknowledged his passion and ability to engage them authentically. They appreciated the curiosity he instilled within them. Yet they couldn't help but feel that there had been a missed opportunity for deeper understanding and personal growth.

Emily, now a senior, contemplated her journey. She realized that while Mr. Fischer's teaching methods had sparked her curiosity, her determination and self-guided exploration allowed her to find meaning in Shakespeare's plays. She envisioned a future where teachers sparked curiosity and facilitated the discovery of personal connections and profound understanding.

Ultimately, Mr. Fischer's dedication and passion made him a beloved teacher. However, his lack of meaning making and personalized support limited the students' potential for transformative learning experiences. This story serves as a reminder that authentic engagement and curiosity stimulation are vital. Still, they must be complemented by meaningful connections and individualized guidance to create a truly transformative educational environment.

Discuss:

How does Mr. Fisher employ or fail to employ the crucial teacher behaviors of authentic engagement, meaning making, personalized support, and stimulating curiosity in his classroom? In what ways do these behaviors contribute to or fail to contribute to an intrinsically motivated learning environment?

Mrs. Jackson

Mrs. Jackson, the eleventh-grade science teacher at Lincoln High School, entered her classroom with a smile that radiated genuine warmth. Her passion for teaching and for her students was evident in how she engaged with them. As she started the day's lesson on cellular biology, she didn't just recite facts and figures. Instead, she shared a personal story about a family member who had battled a disease and how understanding cell functions had played a crucial role in their treatment. The students leaned forward, captivated by her words.

During class discussions, Mrs. Jackson didn't simply provide answers; she encouraged her students to think critically and draw connections. When students struggled to understand concepts, she didn't dismiss their confusion or offer a quick explanation. Instead, she patiently guided them through a series of thought-provoking questions, allowing them to arrive at their own "aha" moment. The joy and sense of accomplishment that lit up their faces were testaments to Mrs. Jackson's skillful guidance.

Mrs. Jackson tried to connect with each student on a personal level outside of class. She took the time to listen, genuinely interested in their thoughts and concerns. When Rihanna, a shy and reserved student, approached her after class, Mrs. Jackson immediately sensed her hesitancy. Sensing Rihanna's struggle with the subject, she offered her support and encouragement. Over time, Mrs. Jackson identified Rihanna's learning style and adapted her teaching approach to accommodate it. She provided resources tailored to Rihanna's needs and recommended relevant books and videos.

As weeks turned into months, Rihanna's confidence began to blossom. Mrs. Jackson's belief in her abilities and the personalized support Rihanna received were transformative. Rihanna's once-limited participation in class discussions turned into active engagement. Her questions became more insightful, demonstrating a deeper understanding of the subject. Mrs. Jackson's eyes twinkled with pride as she watched Rihanna flourish.

Beyond the classroom, Mrs. Jackson's impact was felt in the students' lives. She organized field trips to science labs and invited guest speakers to share their real-world experiences. The students' curiosity sparked as they witnessed science in action, igniting a passion for discovery.

Mrs. Jackson's commitment to meaningful engagement and personalized support had a ripple effect on her students. They developed a thirst for knowledge, driven not by external rewards but by their intrinsic motivation.

Years later, as successful scientists, doctors, and researchers, they would credit Mrs. Jackson for igniting the flame that guided them on their paths.

In the halls of Lincoln High School, Mrs. Jackson's classroom stood as a haven of inspiration and support. Her dedication to showing her students the beauty of science and their potential left an indelible mark on their lives. The legacy of Mrs. Jackson's transformative teaching would continue to inspire generations of students to pursue their dreams and make a lasting impact in the world.

Discuss:

How does Mrs. Jackson employ or fail to employ the teacher behaviors of authentic engagement, meaning making, personalized support, and stimulating curiosity in her classroom? In what ways do these behaviors contribute to or fail to contribute to an intrinsically motivated learning environment?

Section 1C:
Lesson Planning Activities

In the following lesson plans, there is a strong focus on engaging students through authentic and meaningful learning experiences. They encourage the four essential teacher behaviors in addition to active participation, critical thinking, and exploration of topics beyond the classroom. By incorporating various teaching strategies, these lessons aim to cater to students with different learning styles and interests, making the learning process more enjoyable and effective.

Instructions: Use the following examples to guide you in your lesson planning.

Example 1

Grade Level: 7th–12th

Subject: History/Social Studies

Lesson Title: The Emancipation Proclamation

Duration: 60 minutes

Objective:
- Students will actively engage with the history of the Emancipation Proclamation and its significance.
- Students will analyze primary sources and discuss the impact of the Emancipation Proclamation on American society.
- Students will reflect on the importance of authentic engagement, meaning making, personalized support, and stimulating curiosity in historical education.

Materials:
- Primary-source documents related to the Emancipation Proclamation (e.g., excerpts, photographs, political cartoons)
- Whiteboard/flip chart and markers
- Laptops or tablets for research (optional)
- Handouts or worksheets (if needed)

Procedure:

Engage (Authentic Engagement):
- Begin the lesson by asking students: "What do you know about the Emancipation Proclamation? Why do you think it was a significant moment in American history?"
- Allow students to share their prior knowledge and opinions.
- Provide a brief historical context, explaining the background of the Emancipation Proclamation and its connection to the Civil War.

Explore (Meaning Making):
- Divide students into small groups and provide each group with a primary-source document related to the Emancipation Proclamation.
- Instruct students to analyze the document, paying attention to the language, purpose, and potential impact of the Emancipation Proclamation.

- After analyzing the documents, encourage students to discuss within their groups and identify key takeaways and connections to their prior knowledge.
- Facilitate a whole-class discussion, allowing each group to share their findings and insights.

Elaborate (Personalized Support):
- Provide additional information about the Emancipation Proclamation, such as key dates, key figures involved, and its immediate and long-term effects on enslaved people and the United States.
- Address any questions or misconceptions students may have.
- Allow students to work individually or in pairs to conduct further research on specific aspects or individuals related to the Emancipation Proclamation.
- Offer personalized support and guidance to students as they explore their topics of interest.

Evaluate (Stimulating Curiosity):
- Assign students a creative project, such as a presentation, poster, or written reflection, that allows them to showcase their understanding of the Emancipation Proclamation and its significance.
- Encourage students to think critically and consider the broader implications of the Emancipation Proclamation on American society, including ongoing challenges and progress in civil rights.
- Provide resources and references to stimulate curiosity and inspire students' creativity.
- Allow time for students to present or share their projects with the class, fostering curiosity and encouraging peer-to-peer learning.

Closure:
- Summarize the key points discussed during the lesson, emphasizing the significance of the Emancipation Proclamation in American history.
- Reflect on the four teacher behaviors (authentic engagement, meaning making, personalized support, and stimulating curiosity) demonstrated throughout the lesson.

- Engage students in a final class discussion, allowing them to share their reflections on how these behaviors contributed to their understanding of and engagement with the topic.
- Emphasize the importance of studying history with an authentic and meaningful approach to foster curiosity, empathy, and critical thinking.

Extensions:
- Invite students to explore other primary-source documents related to the Emancipation Proclamation or the Civil War and analyze them more thoroughly.
- Organize a debate or role-playing activity where students take on different perspectives (e.g., Abraham Lincoln, enslaved individuals, Northern abolitionists) to understand the complexities of the Emancipation Proclamation.
- Encourage students to research and discuss the ongoing struggles for civil rights in America and their connections to the Emancipation Proclamation.

Assessment:
- Evaluate students' understanding and engagement through class participation, group discussions, and analysis of primary sources.
- Assess students' comprehension and critical thinking skills through their creative projects or written reflections on the significance of the Emancipation Proclamation.

Example 2

Grade Level: 8th

Subject: Health

Lesson Title: The Human Circulatory System

Duration: 60 minutes

Objective:
- Students will understand the structure and function of the human circulatory system.
- Students will explain the importance of a healthy circulatory system for overall well-being.
- Students will engage in activities that promote personalized support and stimulate curiosity about the circulatory system.

Materials:
- Diagrams or models of the human circulatory system
- Whiteboard/flipchart and markers
- Laptops or tablets for research (optional)
- Handouts or worksheets (if needed)

Procedure:

Engage (Authentic Engagement):
- Begin the lesson by asking students: "Have you ever wondered how our bodies transport nutrients and oxygen to different parts? How do you think this process happens?"
- Allow students to share their ideas and discuss their prior knowledge of the circulatory system.
- Share a brief personal story or real-life scenario highlighting the importance of a healthy circulatory system.

Explore (Meaning Making):
- Present a visual representation of the human circulatory system, such as a diagram or model.
- Guide students through a step-by-step exploration of the circulatory system, explaining the main organs and vessels involved (e.g., heart, blood vessels, lungs).

- Facilitate a class discussion, encouraging students to make connections between the circulatory system and the transport of nutrients, oxygen, and waste in the body.
- Use questioning techniques to promote meaning making, such as asking students to explain the purpose of specific components or identify blood flow through the circulatory system.

Elaborate (Personalized Support):
- Provide additional information about the structure and function of the circulatory system, including the different types of blood vessels (arteries, veins, capillaries) and the role of the heart as a pump.
- Address students' questions or misconceptions and offer personalized support to clarify concepts.
- Allow students to work individually or in pairs to research a specific aspect of the circulatory system (e.g., heart health, blood pressure, circulatory diseases).
- Encourage students to take notes, create diagrams, or find real-life examples to deepen their understanding and personalize their learning.

Evaluate (Stimulating Curiosity):
- Conduct a hands-on activity that stimulates curiosity and engages students in exploring the circulatory system further.
- For example, provide stethoscopes or simulated heart rate monitors for students to listen to their heartbeats or measure their pulse before and after physical activity.
- Facilitate a discussion on the observations and encourage students to think critically about how physical activity affects their heart rate and overall circulatory system.
- Invite students to ask questions, make predictions, and propose further investigations related to the circulatory system.

Closure:
- Summarize the key points covered in the lesson, emphasizing the human circulatory system's structure, function, and importance.
- Reflect on the four teacher behaviors (authentic engagement, meaning making, personalized support, and stimulating curiosity) demonstrated throughout the lesson.

- Engage students in a final class discussion, allowing them to share their reflections on how these behaviors contributed to their understanding and engagement with the topic.
- Highlight the significance of maintaining a healthy circulatory system through lifestyle choices and responsible health care.

Extensions:
- Assign a research project where students investigate a specific circulatory system disorder (e.g., hypertension, atherosclerosis) and present their findings to the class.
- Organize a group activity where students create models or diagrams illustrating blood flow through the circulatory system and present them to their peers.
- Encourage students to explore the connection between the circulatory and other body systems (e.g., respiratory and digestive systems) to understand their interdependence.

Assessment:
- Assess students' understanding and engagement through class participation, group discussions, and their ability to explain the structure and function of the circulatory system.
- Evaluate students' research projects, diagrams, or presentations based on the accuracy of information, clarity of explanations, and demonstration of critical thinking skills.

Example 3

Grade Level: 9th–12th

Subject: Geometry

Lesson Title: Exploring the Pythagorean Theorem

Duration: 60 minutes

Objective:
- Students will understand the concept and applications of the Pythagorean theorem.
- Students will apply the Pythagorean theorem to solve real-world and geometric problems.
- Students will engage in activities stimulating curiosity and promoting personalized support in exploring the Pythagorean theorem.

Materials:
- Whiteboard/flip chart and markers
- Pythagorean theorem examples and practice problems
- Geometric shapes (e.g., right-angled triangles)
- Laptops or tablets for online resources (optional)
- Handouts or worksheets (if needed)

Procedure:

Engage (Authentic Engagement):
- Begin the lesson by displaying a right-angled triangle on the board.
- Ask students: "What do you notice about this triangle? How do you think we can find the length of the missing side?"
- Allow students to share their observations and discuss their initial thoughts on solving for the missing side.

Explore (Meaning Making):
- Introduce the Pythagorean theorem, explaining its formula ($a^2 + b^2 = c^2$) and its relevance to right-angled triangles.
- Provide examples of right-angled triangles and guide students through applying the Pythagorean theorem to find the lengths of the missing sides.

- Facilitate a class discussion, encouraging students to explain the meaning of each term in the Pythagorean theorem equation and discuss its implications.

Elaborate (Personalized Support):
- Offer additional examples and practice problems related to the Pythagorean theorem.
- Address students' questions or difficulties and provide personalized support to help them grasp the concept.
- Allow students to work individually or in pairs to solve Pythagorean theorem problems, providing guidance and feedback as needed.
- Encourage students to explore different approaches and strategies for applying the Pythagorean theorem.

Evaluate (Stimulating Curiosity):
- Present real-world scenarios or geometric puzzles that require the use of the Pythagorean theorem to solve.
- Assign a problem-solving activity where students work in groups to design and build structures (e.g., bridges, ramps) that adhere to specific length requirements based on the Pythagorean theorem.
- Encourage students to think critically, make predictions, and test their solutions while applying the Pythagorean theorem.
- Facilitate a class discussion, allowing groups to share their findings, challenges, and creative problem-solving strategies.

Closure:
- Summarize the key points covered in the lesson, emphasizing the concept and applications of the Pythagorean theorem.
- Reflect on the four teacher behaviors (authentic engagement, meaning making, personalized support, and stimulating curiosity) demonstrated throughout the lesson.
- Engage students in a final class discussion, allowing them to share their reflections on how these behaviors contributed to their understanding and engagement with the Pythagorean theorem.
- Highlight the significance of the Pythagorean theorem in various fields, such as architecture, engineering, and navigation.

Extensions:
- Assign a research project where students explore the history and origins of the Pythagorean theorem and its significance in ancient civilizations.
- Organize a "Pythagorean Theorem Challenge" activity where students solve increasingly complex problems or puzzles involving the theorem.
- Encourage students to explore geometric proofs related to the Pythagorean theorem and present their findings to the class.

Assessment:
- Assess students' understanding and engagement through their participation in class discussions, problem-solving activities, and ability to apply the Pythagorean theorem correctly.
- Evaluate students' problem-solving skills and critical thinking through their solutions to real-world scenarios or geometric puzzles involving the Pythagorean theorem.
- Review students' practice problems or worksheets to assess their mastery of the Pythagorean theorem and their ability to solve for missing side lengths.

Example 4

Grade Level: 9th–12th

Subject: Oceanography

Lesson Title: Understanding Ocean Tides

Duration: 60 minutes

Objective:
- Students will understand the causes and characteristics of ocean tides.
- Students will analyze the effects of gravitational forces and the moon-sun relationship on tides.
- Students will engage in activities stimulating curiosity and promoting personalized support in exploring ocean tides.

Materials:
- Whiteboard/flip chart and markers
- Ocean tide charts or online resources
- Models or diagrams of the moon-Earth-sun system
- Laptops or tablets for research (optional)
- Handouts or worksheets (if needed)

Procedure:

Engage (Authentic Engagement):
- Begin the lesson by asking students: "Have you ever noticed how the ocean level changes throughout the day? What do you think causes these changes?"
- Allow students to share their observations and initial thoughts on ocean tides.
- Share a brief personal experience or real-life scenario highlighting the significance of understanding ocean tides.

Explore (Meaning Making):
- Introduce the concept of ocean tides, explaining their connection to the gravitational forces between the moon, Earth, and sun.
- Present models or diagrams of the moon-Earth-sun system to help students visualize the relationships involved in tidal phenomena.

- Facilitate a class discussion, encouraging students to make connections between the positions of the moon, Earth, and sun and the occurrence of high and low tides.
- Use questioning techniques to promote meaning making, such as asking students to explain how the moon's gravitational pull affects tidal patterns.

Elaborate (Personalized Support):
- Provide additional information about the characteristics and variations of ocean tides, including neap tides, spring tides, and tidal ranges.
- Address any questions or difficulties students may have and provide personalized support to help them grasp the concept of ocean tides.
- Allow students to work individually or in pairs to analyze ocean tide charts or conduct online research to identify tidal patterns and their causes in specific locations.
- Encourage students to take notes, create diagrams, or find real-life examples to deepen their understanding and personalize their learning.

Evaluate (Stimulating Curiosity):
- Present real-world scenarios or case studies related to ocean tides, such as the impact of tides on coastal ecosystems or human activities.
- Assign a project or activity where students investigate a specific coastal region or phenomenon affected by ocean tides, such as energy generation or flooding.
- Encourage students to think critically, make predictions, and propose solutions or mitigation strategies related to the effects of ocean tides.
- Facilitate a class discussion, allowing students to share their findings, challenges, and creative problem-solving strategies.

Closure:
- Summarize the key points covered in the lesson, emphasizing the causes, characteristics, and significance of ocean tides.
- Reflect on the four teacher behaviors (authentic engagement, meaning making, personalized support, and stimulating curiosity) demonstrated throughout the lesson.

- Engage students in a final class discussion, allowing them to share their reflections on how these behaviors contributed to their understanding and engagement with ocean tides.
- Highlight the importance of understanding ocean tides in various fields, such as marine navigation, coastal management, and ecological conservation.

Extensions:
- Invite a guest speaker, such as a marine scientist or coastal engineer, to share their expertise and experiences related to ocean tides.
- Organize a field trip to a nearby coastal area or tidal basin where students can observe tidal patterns firsthand and conduct measurements or observations.
- Encourage students to explore the impact of climate change on ocean tides and its implications for coastal communities.

Assessment:
- Assess students' understanding and engagement through participation in class discussions, analysis of tide charts, and completion of assigned projects or activities related to ocean tides.
- Evaluate students' ability to explain the causes and characteristics of ocean tides in written or oral responses.
- Review students' research notes or diagrams to assess their comprehension of tidal phenomena and their ability to connect theoretical concepts to real-world examples.

Lesson Plan Template

This lesson plan template is designed to integrate the four teacher behaviors (authentic engagement, meaning making, personalized support, and stimulating curiosity) into any subject matter for grades 7–12. It provides a flexible structure that can be adapted to suit the specific needs and content of different lessons.

Instructions: Use the following lesson plan template to assist you in creating your unique lessons.

Lesson Plan Template:
Transformational Education

Grade Level: 7th–12th
Subject: [Subject Name]
Lesson Title: [Lesson Title]
Duration: [Duration of the Lesson]
Objective:
- Students will actively engage in authentic learning experiences that foster curiosity and meaning making.
- Students will receive personalized support to meet their needs and develop their potential.
- Students will be stimulated to think critically, ask questions, and explore new ideas.

Materials:
- [List of materials/resources needed for the lesson]

Procedure:

Engage (Authentic Engagement):
- Begin the lesson with a thought-provoking question, a real-life scenario, or a stimulating activity related to the topic.
- Encourage students to share their thoughts, experiences, and opinions.
- Use your own thoughts, experiences, and opinions to engage with the students.
- Create a positive and inclusive learning environment where students feel valued and comfortable expressing their ideas.

Explore (Meaning Making):
- Introduce the key concepts or skills related to the topic.
- Provide opportunities for students to connect their prior knowledge and experiences with the new content.
- Use visual aids, multimedia, or real-world examples to enhance understanding and facilitate meaningful connections.

- Encourage students to ask questions, discuss ideas, and reflect on the significance of the content.

Elaborate (Personalized Support):
- Provide differentiated instruction based on students' needs, learning styles, and abilities.
- Offer one-on-one support, small group discussions, or additional resources to address specific challenges or extend learning for advanced students.
- Regularly check for understanding and provide feedback to guide students' progress.
- Create a supportive and nurturing classroom environment where students feel heard, valued, and empowered.

Evaluate (Stimulating Curiosity):
- Design assessments that require critical thinking, problem-solving, and creative expression.
- Include open-ended questions, projects, or presentations, allowing students to demonstrate their understanding and curiosity.
- Encourage students to reflect on their learning process and set further exploration and growth goals.
- Provide constructive feedback that focuses on developing curiosity, independent thinking, and innovation.

Closure:
- Summarize the key points covered in the lesson and highlight the importance of the four teacher behaviors: authentic engagement, meaning making, personalized support, and stimulating curiosity.
- Encourage students to apply these behaviors in their future learning experiences and daily lives.
- Allow students to ask any remaining questions or share their reflections on the lesson.

Extensions:
- Provide additional resources or activities for students who want to delve deeper into the topic.

- Encourage students to explore related subjects or interdisciplinary connections to broaden their understanding.
- Facilitate opportunities for students to collaborate, share their work, and engage in peer feedback.

Assessment:
- Use formative assessments, such as class discussions, individual reflections, or group activities, to gauge students' understanding and engagement throughout the lesson.
- Use summative assessments, such as projects, presentations, or quizzes, to assess students' mastery of the learning objectives.

The Transformational Education Application Guide *for Groups*

Sections 1D, 1E, 1F, 1G, and 1H are designed to serve *groups* for professional development, department collaboration, coaching, mentoring, or faculty and school-wide initiatives. These sections provide several applications and exercises to help teachers apply the principles of the TE model, which were introduced in the foundational book, *An Introduction to Transformational Education: Redefining Leadership in the Classroom.* These exercises are designed to enhance understanding, promote critical thinking, and provide practical examples for educators. These various applications and exercises in educational theory textbooks aim to bridge the gap between theory and practice, allowing teachers to actively engage with the content and apply it to their teaching contexts.

Section 1D: Reflection and Discussion

Group discussions promote collaboration and knowledge sharing among teachers. They provide opportunities for educators to discuss and debate educational theories, their applications, and their implications for teaching and learning. In this section, we will explore the qualities and practices of transformational educators and leadership, focusing on four key aspects: authentic engagement, meaning making, personalized support, and stimulating curiosity.

Instructions: In your group, take turns sharing your thoughts and experiences. Try to keep the discussion focused on the questions provided. Feel free to take notes during your conversation to share your insights with the larger group later.

Group Reflection Questions: Authentic Engagement
1. How have your experiences as a student shaped your beliefs and practices regarding authentic engagement in the classroom?
2. In what ways can teachers act as role models and demonstrate authentic engagement to inspire students' intrinsic motivation for learning?
3. Reflecting on your teaching practices, how do you incorporate nonverbal cues and genuine reactions to foster authentic engagement and meaningful student interactions?

Group Reflection Questions: Meaning Making
1. How has your experience as a student, particularly concerning meaningful interactions with teachers or mentors, influenced your beliefs about the importance of meaning making in education? Reflect on specific instances or relationships that have shaped your understanding.
2. In what ways do you currently incorporate meaning making in your teaching practices? How do you motivate your students to connect their previous knowledge and experiences with new academic concepts? Share examples of strategies or activities that have effectively fostered meaningful learning experiences for your students.
3. Reflecting on the impact of teacher meaning making on student engagement and sense of community, what steps can you take to enhance your role as a meaning-making leader in the classroom?

How can you align your instructional goals with the values and aspirations of your students to create purpose and intrinsic motivation? Brainstorm specific actions or changes you can implement to cultivate a stronger sense of meaning and collaboration among your students.

Group Reflection Questions: Personalized Support
1. Reflect on when you provided personalized support to a student in your classroom. How did you tailor instruction to meet their individual needs and interests? What were the outcomes of this personalized support regarding the student's growth and motivation?
2. Think about a situation where you may have lacked personalized support for a student. How did this impact the student's experience and motivation? What could you have done differently to demonstrate empathy and individual consideration?
3. Consider the research findings in the text regarding the positive effects of personalized support on student engagement, achievement, and personal adjustment. How do these findings align with your experiences and classroom observations? How can you integrate personalized support into your teaching practices to create a transformational classroom environment?

Group Reflection Questions: Stimulating Curiosity
1. How can you incorporate strategies to stimulate curiosity in your teaching practice? Reflect on specific examples from your own experiences and consider the potential impact on students' thinking and problem-solving skills.
2. Reflecting on the story of Bradley's impact on the author's life, how can you create an intellectually stimulating environment that encourages students to challenge assumptions, take risks, and collaborate? Share an example of a time when you successfully nurtured independent thinking among your students.
3. Consider stimulating curiosity at the leadership level. How can you, as a teacher-leader, foster a sense of curiosity and commitment among your colleagues? Reflect on strategies you can implement to support deep and strategic approaches to learning, resulting in increased student empowerment and growth.

Section 1E:
Peer Mentorship

Having a trusted mentor observe your classroom and offer feedback provides valuable benefits. Their experienced perspective allows for objective observations and constructive criticism, enabling you to gain insights into your teaching practices and areas for improvement. Their guidance helps refine instructional strategies, enhance student engagement, and address specific challenges.

Instructions: Invite a colleague or mentor to utilize this one-to-one observation form. Use the results to boost your professional growth, expand your teaching repertoire, and foster self-reflection.

Authentic Engagement

- The teacher regularly communicates high expectations for student success and provides individual encouragement and support to help students reach their potential.

Y / N | Comments: _____

_____

- The teacher frequently incorporates real-world examples and connections to make learning relevant and meaningful to students' lives.

Y / N | Comments: _____

_____

- The teacher effectively delegates responsibilities to students, empowering them to take ownership of their learning and classroom environment.

Y / N | Comments: _____

_____

- The teacher consistently uses inclusive language and creates opportunities for students to collaborate and engage in meaningful discussions.

Y / N | Comments: _____

_____

- The teacher differentiates instruction based on students' needs and interests, encouraging active participation and curiosity-driven exploration.

Y / N | Comments: _____

_____

- The teacher sparks curiosity by asking thought-provoking questions and encouraging students to explore their inquiries within the subject matter.

Y / N | Comments: _____

_____

- The teacher regularly celebrates students' efforts and growth, emphasizing the joy of learning rather than solely focusing on grades or external rewards.

Y / N | Comments: _____

_____

- The teacher showcases a genuine passion for the subject matter and models a growth mindset, embracing challenges and emphasizing the value of perseverance.

Y / N | Comments: _____

_____

- The teacher consistently demonstrates respect, empathy, and fairness in student interactions, fostering a safe and supportive classroom environment.

Y / N | Comments: _____

_____

- The teacher actively listens to students' ideas and perspectives, encourages respectful discussions, and provides constructive feedback to promote growth and learning.

Y / N | Comments: _____

_____

- The teacher proactively seeks student feedback, adjusts instruction to address individual needs, and creates a positive and inclusive learning environment for all.

Y / N | Comments: _____

_____

Meaning Making

- During class discussions or activities, the teacher shares personal stories or examples that inspire and motivate students to go beyond their ordinary experiences. They may use anecdotes or real-life examples to illustrate how individuals can overcome challenges and achieve extraordinary outcomes.

Y / N | Comments: _____

_____

- At the beginning of each lesson or unit, the teacher communicates the learning goals to the students enthusiastically and engagingly. They may use visual aids, multimedia presentations, or interactive activities to capture students' attention and generate excitement about the upcoming learning experience.

Y / N | Comments: _____

_____

- The teacher frequently facilitates discussions or prompts students to make connections between new knowledge or experiences and their existing knowledge. They encourage students to reflect on their prior understanding and relate it to the current topic. The teacher may ask questions that help students see the relevance and interconnectedness of various concepts.

Y / N | Comments: _____

_____

- The teacher regularly engages students in reflective exercises or discussions where they are encouraged to analyze the meaning and values conveyed by their choices. They provide guidance and prompts to help students think critically about their decisions and consider their actions' ethical, moral, or social implications.

Y / N | Comments: _____

_____

- The teacher structures classroom activities or projects that promote and reinforce prosocial values such as kindness, helping, and cooperation. They actively model and praise acts of kindness, create opportunities for students to collaborate and support each other, and establish a positive and inclusive classroom environment where empathy and cooperation are valued.

Y / N | Comments: _____

_____

- The teacher designs learning experiences that connect students' personal goals and aspirations with the content being taught. They may provide opportunities for students to set individual or collective goals related to the subject matter and help them understand how the knowledge and skills they acquire in class align with their broader life goals.

Y / N | Comments: _____

_____

- The teacher facilitates group projects or activities requiring students to work collaboratively and helpfully. They provide guidance and structure to ensure that students explore and understand prosocial values through their cooperative efforts. The teacher actively intervenes to resolve conflicts or promote positive interactions among students.

Y / N | Comments: _____

_____

- The teacher involves students in the decision-making process within the classroom. They provide opportunities for students to contribute their ideas and opinions regarding class activities, topics, or rules. The teacher listens attentively, acknowledges students' input, and incorporates their suggestions whenever appropriate.

Y / N | Comments: _____

_____

- The teacher creates a classroom environment where students feel cared for and supported. They greet students warmly, use positive and affirming language, and actively listen to students' concerns or needs. The teacher encourages peer support and fosters a sense of belonging by facilitating class discussions or activities that promote inclusivity and respect.

Y / N | Comments: _____

_____

- The teacher consistently demonstrates behaviors that show they genuinely care about students' learning and well-being. They go beyond the required curriculum and provide additional resources, opportunities, or personalized support to enhance students' understanding and engagement. The teacher's enthusiasm, dedication, and encouragement create a meaningful and committed learning atmosphere in the classroom.

Y / N | Comments: _____

_____

Personalized Support
- The teacher greets each student by name and engages in conversations to get to know them personally.

Y / N | Comments: _____

_____

- The teacher differentiates lesson plans to accommodate diverse learning styles and incorporates topics that interest each student.

Y / N | Comments: _____

_____

- The teacher provides individualized feedback and suggestions to help students improve their work and reach their learning goals.

Y / N | Comments: _____

_____

- The teacher showcases and celebrates students' unique talents and abilities through class presentations or recognition.

Y / N | Comments: _____

_____

- The teacher maintains eye contact, nods, and validates students' feelings when they express concerns or share their experiences.

Y / N | Comments: _____

_____

- The teacher gives students choices in their learning, such as selecting topics for projects or deciding how to present their work.

Y / N | Comments: _____

_____

- The teacher creates a classroom environment that encourages collaboration, respect, and positive interactions among students.

Y / N | Comments: _____

_____

- The teacher modifies assignments or instructional materials to ensure they are accessible and challenging for all students.

Y / N | Comments: _____

_____

- The teacher engages in one-on-one conversations with students to understand their interests, hobbies, and experiences outside school.

Y / N | Comments: _____

_____

- The teacher publicly acknowledges and praises students' efforts and contributions in class discussions, written feedback, or certificates of achievement.

Y / N | Comments: _____

_____

Stimulating Curiosity
- The teacher facilitates class discussions that delve into the underlying principles and reasons behind different topics, encouraging students to analyze and question the "how" and "why" aspects. They may also provide examples or case studies that require critical thinking and reflection.

Y / N | Comments: _____

_____

- The teacher creates opportunities for students to explore and solve problems aligned with their interests and curiosities. They design activities or projects that allow students to investigate and find solutions independently, offering resources and guidance as needed.

Y / N | Comments: _____

_____

- The teacher asks thought-provoking questions during class discussions or individual interactions that spark students' intellectual curiosity. These questions challenge conventional thinking, encourage deeper analysis, and invite students to explore alternative perspectives.

Y / N | Comments: _____

_____

- The teacher provides a supportive and nonjudgmental environment that encourages students to express their ideas and opinions freely. They actively listen to students, create a safe space for open discussions, and respect diverse viewpoints without criticism.

Y / N | Comments: _____

_____

- The teacher challenges assumptions and encourages students to think creatively and innovatively. They introduce activities or assignments requiring students to approach problems with originality and offer prompts questioning traditional wisdom.

Y / N | Comments: _____

_____

- The teacher welcomes and embraces new ideas from students, fostering a culture of curiosity and exploration. They create an atmosphere that values and appreciates diverse perspectives, encouraging students to share their unique insights.

Y / N | Comments: _____

_____

- The teacher supports independent thinking among students, allowing them to develop their solutions and approaches. They provide guidance and feedback that promote autonomy, empowering students to take ownership of their learning process.

Y / N | Comments: _____

_____

- The teacher recognizes and affirms students' efforts in stimulating curiosity, creativity, and critical thinking. They provide specific feedback that acknowledges students' contributions and encourages them to continue exploring new ideas.

Y / N | Comments: _____

_____

- The teacher actively seeks to stimulate curiosity across different subjects and activities in the classroom. They introduce new topics, learning resources, or hands-on experiences that ignite curiosity and promote interdisciplinary connections.

Y / N | Comments: _____

_____

- The teacher firmly believes that stimulating curiosity in the classroom increases affective and cognitive growth for students. They consistently communicate this belief and may share relevant research findings, personal anecdotes, or inspirational stories to reinforce the value of curiosity in learning and development.

Please feel free to add comments or observations as they apply:

Y / N | Comments: _____

Section 1F: Scenario

This section presents a specific teaching scenario and asks teachers to apply the theories and strategies they have learned to address the challenges or opportunities presented. They encourage teachers to think critically, make informed decisions, and consider the practical implications of the theories.

Instructions: Read the following hypothetical scenario that teachers may encounter in their classrooms. Utilize the discussion questions to analyze the situation, identify challenges, and propose solutions based on the theories and concepts discussed in the textbook.

Scenario

Once upon a time, a dedicated teacher named Mr. Keller was instructing in a small town. He had a passion for teaching and believed in the power of education to transform lives. Mr. Keller was a tenth-grade Introduction to Business teacher at Lincoln High School. He not only taught his subject matter but also demonstrated the behaviors of a transformational educator.

One of Mr. Keller's students, Jimmy, was a talented football player. Mr. Keller recognized Jimmy's potential and tried to engage him authentically. He incorporated examples from the sports industry into his lessons and encouraged Jimmy to explore business opportunities within the field of athletics. Jimmy felt a connection with the subject matter and developed a greater appreciation for learning beyond the football field.

Sarah, a dedicated tenth-grade student, had an unwavering passion for dance. Recognizing her love for the arts, Mr. Keller went the extra mile to make his lessons more engaging and relevant. He integrated dance-related examples into his lectures and arranged for a professional dancer to visit the class and share their experiences. Inspired by Mr. Keller's genuine interest in her passion, Sarah felt supported and validated. She found the motivation to excel academically, knowing that her teacher valued her artistic pursuits just as much as her academic growth.

Jenna was a student who loved video games. Mr. Keller saw the potential in gamification and used it to stimulate Jenna's curiosity in business concepts. He created interactive lessons that allowed students to apply business strategies within virtual game environments. Jenna became actively engaged in her learning, and her passion for video games translated into a passion for business.

Sam, on the other hand, was apathetic toward school. Mr. Keller recognized Sam's disinterest and took the time to understand his individual needs. He provided personalized support by offering one-on-one guidance and encouragement. Mr. Keller showed empathy and helped Sam find relevance in the subject matter by relating it to Sam's interests. Sam's apathy gradually transformed into motivation, and he began actively participating in class.

Through his authentic engagement, meaning making, personalized support, and stimulating curiosity, Mr. Keller created a positive and transformative learning environment for his students. Jimmy, Sarah, Jenna, and Sam experienced greater connection, well-being, and motivation in Mr. Keller's class. They learned business concepts and developed essential life skills and a love for learning.

Years later, Jimmy became a successful entrepreneur in the sports industry, Sarah pursued a career as a professional dancer, Jenna started her own video game development company, and Sam discovered his passion for education and became a teacher. Mr. Keller's positive influence spread through these students' lives and influenced their choices and successes.

Mr. Keller's commitment to being a transformational educator had a lasting impact on his students. His genuine care, support, and belief in their potential inspired them to reach their goals and pursue their dreams. The legacy of Mr. Keller's teaching behaviors continued to shape the lives of his students for years to come.

Group Discussion:

Take a few moments to read the scenario above about Mr. Keller, a transformational educator who successfully applied the four teacher behaviors (authentic engagement, meaning making, personalized support, and stimulating curiosity). Reflecting on your content area and grade level, discuss how you could apply these four teacher behaviors to create a transformative learning environment for your students.

Authentic Engagement:
- How can you authentically engage students in your content area? Share specific strategies or activities that can ignite their interest and make learning meaningful.
- How can you avoid relying solely on external motivators (rewards, grades) and foster internal motivation for students to value learning for its merits?

Meaning Making:
- In what ways can you help students make connections between your content area and their personal lives, interests, or goals?
- How can you inspire curiosity and encourage students to explore the meaning and value of their learning concepts?

Personalized Support:
- How can you provide individual consideration for each student in your classroom? Share practical ways to address their unique needs, interests, and abilities.

- How can you demonstrate empathy and create a supportive environment that fosters student growth and intrinsic motivation?

Stimulating Curiosity:
- How can you create opportunities for students to think critically, ask questions, and engage in problem-solving related to your content area?
- What strategies can you employ to ignite curiosity and inspire independent thinking among your students?

Share your thoughts, ideas, and experiences with the group. Let's explore how we can apply these four teacher behaviors to empower our students and create transformative learning experiences in our classrooms.

Section 1G: Role-Playing

Role-Playing Exercises:

Role-playing activities allow teachers to simulate instructional scenarios or interactions with students. Use the following role-playing exercises to assist you in exploring different teaching approaches, experimenting with strategies, and gaining insights into the practical applications of educational theories.

Role-Play 1

Title: Engaging a Disengaged Student with Vocational Aspirations

Objective: To demonstrate how Mrs. Field, a teacher, can utilize one or more teacher behaviors (authentic engagement, meaning making, personalized support, and stimulating curiosity) to engage Larry, a disengaged student with vocational aspirations, and help him see the value of the academic subject.

Scenario: Mrs. Field is a teacher in a high school classroom, and she notices that her student, Larry, is consistently disengaged and fails to see the value of the academic subject. Larry aspires to be a diesel mechanic and believes that the academic subject is irrelevant to his career goal. Mrs. Field's goal is to connect with Larry, demonstrate the importance of the academic subject to his vocational aspirations, and engage him through one or more teacher behaviors.

Instructions:
- Set up the classroom for a typical classroom setting. Begin the exercise with the following scenario:
- Teacher (Mrs. Field): Start the class by greeting the students and introducing the topic for the day, which may seem unrelated to Larry's vocational aspirations.
- Larry: Displays disengaged behavior, such as a lack of interest and relevance to his future career as a diesel mechanic.
- Choose one or more teacher behaviors (authentic engagement, meaning making, personalized support, or stimulating curiosity) to address Larry's disengagement and help him see the value of the academic subject. Use the following examples:

Authentic Engagement:
- Mrs. Field: Begin the class by sharing a real-life example illustrating how knowledge of the academic subject can be valuable to a diesel mechanic. For instance, explain how understanding the principles of physics or mathematics can help optimize the performance of diesel engines or troubleshoot complex mechanical issues.
- Larry: Starts showing interest and realizing the relevance of the academic subject to his vocational aspirations.

Meaning Making:
- Mrs. Field: Connect the academic subject to Larry's future career as a diesel mechanic by explaining how foundational knowledge in various subjects can contribute to his success. For example, highlight the importance of critical thinking, problem-solving skills, and effective communication, which are essential qualities for any professional, including diesel mechanics.
- Larry: Starts recognizing the value of the academic subject in developing crucial skills for his chosen profession.

Personalized Support:
- Mrs. Field: Have a one-on-one conversation with Larry, showing genuine interest in his career aspirations as a diesel mechanic. Share success stories of individuals who have integrated their academic knowledge with their vocational pursuits, highlighting how a strong foundation in different subjects can lead to career advancements and opportunities.
- Larry: Feels supported and begins to appreciate how the academic subject can contribute to his future success as a diesel mechanic.

Stimulating Curiosity:
- Mrs. Field: Incorporate practical examples or case studies that showcase the application of the academic subject in real-life situations related to diesel mechanics. Encourage Larry to explore and analyze these examples, fostering his curiosity and highlighting the relevance of the subject matter to his vocational aspirations.
- Larry: Becomes curious and actively engages in class discussions, recognizing the practicality and importance of the academic subject to his chosen career path.

Conduct the exercise for approximately five minutes, focusing on implementing the chosen teacher behavior(s) to engage Larry and help him see the value of the academic subject.

Discuss:
- Conclude the exercise by summarizing the key points covered during the brief interaction and encouraging Larry to increase engagement and understanding of the subject's relevance.

- Reflect as a group on the effectiveness of the chosen teacher behavior(s) in engaging Larry and discuss other strategies that could be employed to further support his involvement in the academic subject while aligning with his vocational aspirations.

Note: This exercise demonstrates a brief interaction where a teacher engages a disengaged student with vocational aspirations. In reality, it may require ongoing efforts and support to fully address a student's disengagement and help them see the value of the academic subject within the context of their career goals.

Role-Play 2

Title: Engaging a Socially Anxious Student through Supportive Language Learning

Objective: To demonstrate how Mr. Barker, a Spanish teacher, can utilize one or more teacher behaviors (authentic engagement, meaning making, personalized support, and stimulating curiosity) to engage Niara, a socially anxious ninth-grade track and field athlete, and create a supportive environment for language learning despite her anxiety.

Scenario: Mr. Barker teaches a ninth-grade Spanish course, and he notices that Niara, one of his students, struggles with intense social anxiety. Niara finds it challenging to participate actively in class due to her fear. Additionally, Mr. Barker has a student teacher assisting him this year, and he grades student participation at 25%. Mr. Barker aims to connect with Niara, provide personalized support, and create a safe and engaging classroom environment, encouraging her to participate in Spanish language learning.

Instructions: Set up the classroom for a typical Spanish language learning environment, incorporating visuals and interactive resources. Begin the exercise with the following scenario:

- Teacher (Mr. Barker): Start the class by greeting the students and introducing the topic for the day, which includes interactive speaking activities.
- Niara: Displays signs of social anxiety, such as avoiding eye contact, appearing tense, and hesitating to participate in class discussions.
- Choose one or more teacher behaviors (authentic engagement, meaning making, personalized support, or stimulating curiosity) to address Niara's social anxiety and create a supportive language learning environment. Use the following examples:

Authentic Engagement:
- Mr. Barker: Begin the class by sharing a personal story or experience related to language learning struggles, emphasizing that making mistakes is a natural part of the learning process. Encourage a non-judgmental classroom atmosphere where everyone is supported and encouraged to take risks.

- Niara: Starts feeling more at ease, realizing that language learning involves growth and learning from mistakes.

Meaning Making:
- Mr. Barker: Explain the importance of language learning in broadening horizons, connecting with different cultures, and fostering empathy. Share examples of how Spanish language skills can enhance future opportunities and interactions, both academically and personally.
- Niara: Begins to understand the relevance of language learning beyond the classroom and feels motivated to engage in the subject.

Personalized Support:
- Mr. Barker: Talk privately with Niara, expressing genuine concern for her well-being and understanding her social anxiety. Discuss strategies to alleviate stress during classroom activities, such as offering alternative participation options (written responses, small group discussions, etc.) or implementing a buddy system for support.
- Niara: Feels supported and appreciated, knowing that her teacher understands her challenges and is willing to accommodate her needs.

Stimulating Curiosity:
- Mr. Barker: Design interactive language learning activities that encourage collaborative learning, such as group projects or paired role-plays. Frame these activities as opportunities to learn from and support each other, fostering a sense of camaraderie among the students.
- Niara: Becomes curious about Spanish language and culture, feeling motivated to participate in activities that provide opportunities for collaborative learning rather than focusing solely on individual performance.

Conduct the exercise for approximately five minutes, focusing on implementing the chosen teacher behavior(s) to engage Niara and create a supportive language learning environment.

Discuss:
- Conclude the exercise by summarizing the key points covered during the brief interaction and encouraging Niara for her willingness to participate and engage in the Spanish language learning process.
- Reflect on the effectiveness of the chosen teacher behavior(s) in engaging Niara and fostering a supportive language learning environment. Discuss other strategies that could be employed to support her involvement further and reduce social anxiety in the classroom.

Note: This exercise demonstrates a brief interaction where a teacher engages a socially anxious student in a language learning setting. Creating an ongoing support system for students with social anxiety is important, involving collaboration with school counselors or professionals who can provide further guidance and assistance.

Section 1H: Interdisciplinary and Collaborative Lesson Planning

Cross-Curricular Lessons

Creating cross-curricular lessons for ninth to twelfth grade based on the principles of authentic engagement, meaning making, personalized support, and stimulating curiosity can foster a holistic and transformative educational experience. Here are some ideas on how an entire faculty could incorporate these behaviors into their lessons:

Authentic Engagement:
- **English and Social Studies:** Engage students in a project-based learning activity where they research and analyze a historical event or literary work that resonates with current social issues. Encourage them to express their perspectives authentically and discuss the impact of the event or work on society.
- **Science and Art:** Integrate scientific concepts and artistic expression by having students conduct experiments and create visual representations or multimedia presentations that convey their findings and interpretations. Emphasize the importance of genuine curiosity and self-driven exploration.

Meaning Making:
- **Math and History:** Explore the historical context of mathematical concepts, such as the development of calculus or the use of statistics in analyzing historical data. Help students understand the significance of these concepts in different historical periods and their impact on society.
- **Foreign Language and Literature:** Connect the study of literature in a foreign language with cultural understanding. Encourage students to analyze literary works from different periods and regions, emphasizing the cultural, historical, and social significance embedded in the texts.

Personalized Support:
- **Physical Education and Health:** Design individualized fitness plans considering students' unique needs, interests, and fitness levels. Provide ongoing support and guidance to help students achieve their personal goals and develop lifelong habits of physical well-being.
- **Career and Technical Education (CTE) and Mathematics:** Integrate mathematics into practical, real-world scenarios relevant to different career pathways. Help students understand the mathematical concepts and calculations involved in their chosen fields, providing personalized support to strengthen their skills.

Stimulating Curiosity:
- **Science and Technology**: Engage students in inquiry-based projects where they investigate real-world problems or phenomena. Encourage them to explore, ask questions, design experiments, and propose innovative solutions, fostering a spirit of curiosity and critical thinking.
- **Music and Literature:** Introduce students to different genres of music and challenge them to analyze the lyrics, themes, and emotions conveyed in the songs. Encourage students to connect the music with literary works with similar themes or messages, stimulating their curiosity about the interplay between different art forms.

These are examples of how authentic engagement, meaning making, personalized support, and stimulating curiosity can be applied in ninth to twelfth-grade cross-curricular lessons. By incorporating these behaviors into their teaching practices, the faculty can create a transformative learning environment that inspires students, fosters their holistic development, and prepares them for future success.

Cross-Curricular Lesson 1:

Title: The Spanish-American War and Its Impact

Subjects: English, Social Studies, Science, Art

Grade Level: 9th–12th

Objective: Students will explore the causes, events, and consequences of the Spanish-American War through a multidisciplinary approach, integrating English, social studies, science, and art.

Duration: 3–4 class periods

Materials:
- Access to textbooks, articles, or online resources on the Spanish-American War
- Maps and historical documents related to the war
- Art supplies (paper, pencils, markers, paints, etc.)
- Optional: multimedia resources, primary sources, videos, or documentaries related to the war

Procedure:

Introduction (Social Studies):
- Begin by providing an overview of the Spanish-American War, its causes, and the geopolitical context of the time.
- Engage students in a class discussion about the motivations, key events, and impact of the war on the United States, Spain, and other regions involved.

Research and Analysis (English):
- Divide students into small groups and assign each group a specific aspect or event of the Spanish-American War to research (e.g., the sinking of the USS *Maine*, the Battle of San Juan Hill, the Treaty of Paris, the role of yellow journalism, etc.).
- Instruct students to gather information from various sources, including primary and secondary texts, to analyze and synthesize the information.

Scientific Exploration (Science):
- Focus on the impact of the war on public health and environmental factors.
- Explore the role of diseases, such as yellow fever and malaria, during the war. Discuss how scientific advancements in medicine and sanitation helped combat these diseases.
- Engage students in a discussion about the ecological consequences of the war, such as deforestation, pollution, or changes in biodiversity. Analyze how these changes affected local ecosystems and communities.

Creative Expression (Art):
- Encourage students to create visual representations that depict significant aspects of the war, such as critical battles, political cartoons, propaganda posters, or portraits of prominent figures.
- Provide art supplies and allow students to choose their preferred medium (drawing, painting, collage, etc.) to bring their ideas to life.
- Emphasize using artistic elements like color, composition, and symbolism to convey historical events and themes related to the war.

Culminating Activity (English, Social Studies, Art):
- Have each group present their research findings and artistic creations to the class.
- Instruct students to prepare short presentations that include a summary of their research, the significance of their assigned topic, and an explanation of their artistic choices.
- Facilitate a class discussion where students reflect on the interconnectedness of the different aspects studied and the overall impact of the Spanish-American War.

Extension:
- Students can write historical fiction or journalistic articles from the perspective of individuals involved in the war.
- Organize a debate or mock trial, where students assume different roles and argue for or against US intervention in the conflict.

- Encourage students to explore additional artistic forms related to the war, such as music or poetry, and perform or share their creations with the class.

Assessment:
- Research notes and presentations
- Artistic creations and accompanying artist statements
- Participation in class discussions and presentations
- Written reflections or essays on the impact and significance of the Spanish-American War

Cross-Curricular Lesson 2:

Title: Exploring Lacrosse through Physical Education, Mathematics, Social Studies, and French

Subjects: Physical Education and Health, Mathematics, Social Studies, French

Grade Level: 9th-12th

Objective: Students will engage in a comprehensive study of the game of lacrosse, integrating physical activity, mathematical analysis, historical and cultural perspectives, and language learning.

Duration: 3-4 class periods

Materials:
- Lacrosse equipment (sticks, balls, protective gear, etc.)
- Whiteboard or chart paper
- Maps or globes
- Computer or tablet with internet access
- French vocabulary resources (dictionaries, flashcards, etc.)

Procedure:

Introduction to Lacrosse (Physical Education and Health, Social Studies):
- Begin with a brief history of lacrosse, highlighting its origins and cultural significance among Indigenous peoples of North America.
- Discuss the basic rules and objectives of the game, emphasizing teamwork, coordination, and physical fitness.
- Show images or videos of lacrosse gameplay, including traditional Indigenous forms of the sport and modern variations.

Lacrosse Skills and Fitness (Physical Education and Health):
- Engage students in a warm-up session to prepare for lacrosse activities.
- Teach fundamental lacrosse skills, such as passing, catching, cradling, and shooting.
- Organize drills and small-sided games focusing on skill development, teamwork, and fitness components such as agility, speed, and endurance.

Mathematical Analysis of Lacrosse (Mathematics):
- Introduce students to statistical analysis and mathematical concepts related to lacrosse.
- Explain how data such as goals scored, assists, and shooting percentages can be collected and used to analyze player performance and team strategies.
- Provide actual game data or hypothetical scenarios for students to calculate and interpret statistics, create graphs, and make predictions.

Lacrosse around the World (Social Studies, French):
- Discuss the global spread of lacrosse and its cultural significance in different countries.
- Introduce students to the international lacrosse community, including national teams and major tournaments.
- Assign students to research and present information about lacrosse in a specific country or region, including its history, current status, and notable players.
- Integrate French language learning by having students present their findings in French, using appropriate vocabulary and phrases related to lacrosse.

Culminating Activity (Physical Education and Health, Mathematics, Social Studies, French):
- Organize a mini lacrosse tournament where students apply their skills and strategic understanding of the game.
- Use the statistical data collected during the games to analyze and compare team performances, calculate individual player statistics, and discuss the results mathematically.
- Facilitate a class discussion on lacrosse's cultural and historical aspects in different regions, drawing connections between the sport and social studies concepts.
- Encourage students to use French vocabulary related to lacrosse during gameplay and discussions.

Extension:
- Invite a guest speaker, such as a lacrosse coach, player, or Indigenous community member, to share their experiences and knowledge of the sport.
- Research and compare traditional Indigenous lacrosse games with modern versions, discussing the cultural significance and adaptations over time.
- Explore the biomechanics and physics of lacrosse, analyzing the forces involved in passing, shooting, and ball movement.

Assessment:
- Participation and skill demonstration during lacrosse activities
- Mathematical analysis of lacrosse statistics and interpretations
- Research presentations on lacrosse in different countries or regions
- Use of French vocabulary and language proficiency during discussions and presentations

Cross-Curricular Lesson 3:

Title: *I Will Always Write Back: How One Letter Changed Two Lives*

Grade Level: 9th–12th

Duration: 4–5 class periods

Subjects: English, Social Studies, Mathematics, Geography

Objectives:
- Analyze the themes and cultural perspectives in the book *I Will Always Write Back*.
- Explore the historical, geographical, and social contexts of the book.
- Develop empathy and cross-cultural understanding through the study of personal narratives.
- Apply mathematical and geographical skills to enhance comprehension and critical thinking.

Materials:
- Copies of the book *I Will Always Write Back: How One Letter Changed Two Lives* by Caitlin Alifirenka, Liz Welch, Martin Ganda
- Whiteboard or chart paper
- Maps or globes
- Art supplies (optional)

Procedure:

Introduction:
- Engage students in a discussion about the importance of personal narratives and the impact of cultural exchange.
- Introduce the book *I Will Always Write Back* and its friendship, empathy, poverty, and global connections themes.
- Highlight the objectives of the lesson and the cross-curricular nature of the study.

English:
- Assign students to read the book *I Will Always Write Back* individually or in small groups.
- Discuss the book's themes, character development, and author's purpose.

- Analyze significant quotes or passages that illustrate cultural differences, socioeconomic challenges, or personal growth.

Social Studies:
- Explore the historical and social contexts of the book.
- Provide background information on Zimbabwe and the United States during the period covered in the book.
- Discuss both countries' socio-political factors, economic challenges, and educational systems.
- Engage students in discussions about poverty, access to education, and global inequality.

Mathematics:
- Integrate mathematical analysis into the study of the book.
- Ask students to analyze and interpret data presented in the book, such as Martin's family's income and expenses.
- Explore mathematical concepts related to budgeting, currency conversion, or financial literacy.
- Engage students in discussions or problem-solving activities that require mathematical reasoning and critical thinking.

Geography:
- Investigate the geographical settings of the book.
- Use maps, globes, or online resources to locate and study Zimbabwe and the United States.
- Analyze each location's geographical features, climate, culture, and population.
- Discuss the impact of geography on the characters' lives and experiences.

Culminating Activity:
- Ask students to visually represent a significant scene, character, or theme from the book.
- Encourage them to use art supplies to create drawings, paintings, collages, or multimedia presentations.
- Provide time for students to present and explain their artwork, emphasizing the connections between their visual representation and the cross-curricular themes studied.

Assessment:
- Assess students' comprehension through class discussions, participation, and written reflections on the book's themes and cultural perspectives.
- Evaluate students' understanding of mathematical concepts through problem-solving activities or assessments related to the book's financial aspects.
- Assess students' geographical knowledge through map quizzes, presentations, or written responses.

Extension:
- Encourage students to research and explore other personal narratives or books that discuss cultural exchange and global issues.
- Connect the book's themes to current events or real-world scenarios, fostering critical thinking and empathy.

Note: Teachers can modify the lesson based on their students' specific needs and grade levels. They can also integrate additional subjects or activities as deemed appropriate. It is crucial to align the lesson with curriculum standards and learning goals in each subject area.

This lesson plan template integrates the four teacher behaviors (authentic engagement, meaning making, personalized support, stimulating curiosity) into a cross-curricular lesson for any subject in grades 7–12. It provides a flexible structure that can be adapted to suit the specific needs and content of different lessons.

Cross-Curricular Lesson Template

Title:

Grade Level:

Duration:

Subjects:

Objectives:

Materials:

Procedure:

Introduction:
- Engage students by providing an overview of the topic or theme that will be explored across multiple subjects.
- Introduce the lesson's objectives and the connection between the different subject areas involved.

Subject Area 1:
- Provide an activity or lesson plan that aligns with the objectives of subject area 1.
- Include instructions, materials needed, and any specific guidelines for implementation.
- Integrate relevant content from other subject areas to reinforce connections.

Subject Area 2:
- Provide an activity or lesson plan that aligns with the objectives of subject area 2.
- Include instructions, materials needed, and any specific guidelines for implementation.
- Incorporate cross-curricular connections and encourage students to connect with previous and upcoming subjects.

Subject Area 3:
- Provide an activity or lesson plan that aligns with the objectives of subject area 3.

- Include instructions, materials needed, and any specific guidelines for implementation.
- Promote interdisciplinary connections and encourage students to apply knowledge and skills from other subject areas.

Subject Area 4:
- Provide an activity or lesson plan that aligns with the objectives of subject area 4.
- Include instructions, materials needed, and any specific guidelines for implementation.
- Foster cross-curricular understanding and engagement, encouraging students to apply concepts and skills from different subjects.

Culminating Activity:
- Design a culminating activity that integrates the learning from all subject areas.
- Provide clear instructions and guidelines for the activity, including any collaborative or individual components.
- Emphasize the application of knowledge and skills across subjects and encourage critical thinking and creativity.

Assessment:
- Outline assessment methods to evaluate students' understanding and achievement of the objectives.
- Include criteria or rubrics for assessing both subject-specific knowledge and interdisciplinary connections.
- Provide opportunities for self-reflection and peer feedback.

Extension:
- Suggest additional activities or resources for students who want to explore the topic further or take on different challenges.
- Offer ideas for extension activities that promote independent research, project-based learning, or real-world applications.

Note: This template provides a framework for creating cross-curricular lessons involving multiple subject areas. Teachers can adapt and modify it to suit their teaching contexts, grade levels, and subjects. Ensuring that the objectives and activities align with the curriculum standards and learning goals of each subject area involved is essential.

Chapter 2

Cultivating School Climate

This chapter contains several exercises and applications to help teachers apply the theoretical content found in chapter 2 of the accompanying foundational text, *An Introduction to Transformational Education*. These exercises are designed to enhance understanding, promote critical thinking, and provide practical examples for educators. These various applications and exercises in educational theory textbooks aim to bridge the gap between theory and practice, allowing teachers to actively engage with the content and apply it to their teaching contexts.

- **Section 2A: Self-Assessment and Reflection**
- **Section 2B: Case Studies**
- **Section 2C: Lesson Planning Activities**
- **Section 2D: Reflection and Discussion**
- **Section 2E: Peer Mentorship**
- **Section 2F: Scenarios**
- **Section 2G: Role-Playing**
- **Section 2H: Interdisciplinary and Collaborative Lesson Planning**

Section 2A:
Self-Assessment and Reflection

The School Climate Self-Assessment is a tool that allows educators to evaluate their teaching practices and assess their school climate. This activity provides self-assessment prompts to help teachers reflect on their instructional practices, beliefs, and professional growth. It will encourage educators to evaluate their strengths, identify improvement areas, and set further development goals. **This self-assessment consists of three sections: Classroom Support, School Kindness, and Aesthetic Guidance.** Each section contains a series of statements related to the respective category.

School Climate Self-Assessment

Instructions: For each statement, indicate your agreement level or practice frequency.

5—Strongly Agree, 4—Agree, 3—Neutral, 2—Disagree, 1—Strongly Disagree

Classroom Support

Classroom support and empowerment are key to a thriving learning environment. This self-assessment helps you reflect on your role in fostering empathy, care, and holistic development. By evaluating your practices, you'll identify strengths and areas for improvement, contributing to a classroom that empowers every student.

_____ 1. I actively strive to understand and share the feelings of my students.

_____ 2. I demonstrate compassion and sensitivity toward the challenges and experiences of my students.

_____ 3. I show care toward my students through my words and actions.

_____ 4. I prioritize their well-being and foster a nurturing classroom environment. I provide the necessary support and resources to help students succeed academically and socio-emotionally.

_____ 5. I promote peer support and encourage students to care for and support one another.

_____ 6. I involve students in decision-making processes within the classroom.

_____ 7. I am aware of the impact of peer support on student connectedness to school and socio-emotional well-being.

_____ 8. I actively foster a positive peer support system in the classroom.

_____ 9. I implement strategies and activities that promote social and emotional growth among my students.

_____ 10. I actively work toward strengthening the moderating relationship between my teaching behaviors and student outcomes.

Classroom Support Total Score _____/50

School Kindness

Kindness is key to creating a positive and supportive learning environment. This self-assessment allows you to reflect on how often you practice kindness and demonstrate genuine concern for others' well-being.

_____ 1. I actively engage in voluntary acts of kindness toward my fellow students, teachers, and staff members.

_____ 2. I genuinely care about the well-being and emotional health of others in the school community.

_____ 3. I believe that creating a culture of school kindness stems from a genuine desire to help and benefit others and is not motivated by external rewards or punishments.

_____ 4. I believe practicing school kindness contributes to a positive school climate and enhances the socio-emotional well-being of students.

_____ 5. I believe that school kindness positively impacts students' life satisfaction and academic self-efficacy.

_____ 6. I actively strive to improve the social wellness of the school community through my kind actions and behaviors.

_____ 7. I believe that school kindness can foster healthy interpersonal relationships and promote prosocial behaviors among students, staff, and community members.

_____ 8. I believe that school kindness plays a role in enhancing students' cognitive, behavioral, and emotional engagement in their education.

_____ 9. I actively participate in creating a classroom environment where kindness and caring behaviors are valued and promoted.

_____ 10. I recognize the importance of school kindness and its role in the Transformational Education model for creating a positive and supportive educational environment.

School Kindness Total Score _____/50

Aesthetic Guidance

The classroom environment is essential in promoting student engagement, creativity, and well-being. This self-assessment encourages you to reflect on your approach to aesthetics in education, from the use of beauty and art to the thoughtful arrangement of space. By evaluating your responses, you'll gain insights into your commitment to creating a sensory-rich, empowering, and stimulating learning environment.

_____ 1. I believe in the importance of creating a visually appealing classroom environment.

_____ 2. I incorporate elements of beauty and art in my classroom design.

_____ 3. I pay attention to the overall aesthetics of the classroom, including colors, lighting, and organization.

_____ 4. I actively seek ways to engage students' senses through the physical arrangement of the classroom.

_____ 5. I provide opportunities for students to make choices and have a sense of freedom within the classroom.

_____ 6. I create an environment that allows students to distance themselves emotionally from things that may hinder their learning.

_____ 7. I encourage students to explore and discover new connections in the classroom.

_____ 8. I believe that aesthetic experiences positively impact students' well-being and academic performance.

_____ 9. I continuously strive to improve the aesthetic quality of my classroom.

_____ 10. I know the research linking aesthetic experiences to critical thinking and problem-solving skills.

Aesthetic Guidance Total Score _____/50

Interpretation of Scores by Section:

Scoring:
- Add up your scores for all the statements.
- The higher the total score, the more you are currently integrating and promoting elements of school climate in your teaching and classroom environment.

Interpretation:
- 41–50: You effectively incorporate the target teacher behavior strategies in your classroom.
- 31–40: Your use of the target teacher behavior in the classroom is moderate. Continue to build on your current strategies to enhance this behavior.
- 21–30: You have some level of the target teacher behavior in your classroom, but there is room for improvement.
- 10–20: Your use of the target teacher behavior in the classroom may be limited.

Note: This self-assessment tool is designed to indicate your current use of the Transformational Education target for the classroom or school context. It is not a comprehensive evaluation and should be used as a starting point for reflection and professional growth.

Individual Reflection Questions
Transformational Education and School Climate

In education, we embark on a journey of profound influence, shaping not just academic growth but the essence of our students' lives. As we delve into the intricate tapestry of school climate, we discover its pivotal role in nurturing an environment where students flourish. These introspective inquiries are a compass, guiding us to reflect upon our transformative actions as educators and their resounding echoes within the school's atmosphere.

Instructions: Utilize the following questions to reflect on your current practices regarding school climate as described in chapter 2 of *An Introduction to Transformational Education*. You are encouraged to write your thoughts down for later reflection and discussion with a mentor.

1. Consider the influence of different school options and educational contexts on the school climate. How do you think these variations impact your role as a teacher and the overall atmosphere in the school?
2. How do your behaviors as a teacher shape the school climate? Can you provide specific examples demonstrating your actions' impact on the overall environment?
3. Ponder the significance of school climate as a moderating variable. How does the school climate, including teacher behaviors, administration, and staff attitudes, affect the relationship between your teaching practices and student outcomes? Can you recall instances where the school climate altered the direction or strength of this relationship?
4. Explore the importance of classroom support in fostering a positive school climate. How do your empathetic and caring behaviors toward students contribute to their academic performance and socio-emotional well-being? Can you think of specific examples that highlight the influence of your support?
5. Contemplate the role of school kindness in enhancing students' social wellness. How do intentional acts of kindness positively impact the classroom and school environment?

6. Reflect on instances where acts of kindness have fostered positive relationships among students, staff, and community members. How have you observed acts of kindness influencing students' confidence in their abilities and overall learning engagement? Can you share examples of how kindness has affected students' well-being?
7. Reflect on the impact of aesthetic guidance on the school climate and student experiences. How have specific physical elements within your classroom or school space influenced students' learning behavior and achievement? Can you recall instances where favorable aesthetics contributed to improved outcomes?
8. Consider the concept of aesthetics in education and its relationship to critical thinking, creativity, and problem-solving skills. How have you witnessed the influence of favorable aesthetic experiences on students' ability to think critically and creatively? Can you provide examples where aesthetics enhanced student performance?
9. Evaluate your role as a transformational teacher leader within a supportive, kind, and aesthetically guided school climate. How have you demonstrated Transformational Leadership behaviors, and how have they contributed to tangible benefits for your students? Can you provide specific examples showcasing the positive outcomes of teacher leadership and a positive school climate?
10. Reflect on the four dimensions of aesthetic experience (object directness, felt freedom, detached affect, and active discovery) and their alignment with the Transformational Education model. How have you incorporated these dimensions into your teaching practices to enhance students' aesthetic experiences? Can you share how these experiences have positively impacted student well-being and performance?

Section 2B:
Case Studies

Case studies present real or hypothetical scenarios teachers may encounter in their classrooms. They require educators to analyze the situation, identify challenges, and propose solutions based on the theories and concepts discussed in the textbook.

Instructions: Read the provided case studies carefully. Take note of the critical points and details presented in the text. Aim to arrive at well-rounded and thoughtful answers that consider various perspectives. Refer to the case study as needed to support your responses.

Mr. Williams

Mr. Williams, a social studies teacher at Lincoln High School, walked into his classroom with a warm smile, greeting each student by name. He took the time to listen to their concerns, showing genuine empathy for their struggles. When a student felt discouraged, he would offer encouragement and support, creating an atmosphere of trust and understanding.

Mr. Williams encouraged students to participate and share their ideas during group discussions. He fostered a sense of community by valuing each student's opinion and involving them in decision-making. Students felt a strong connection with their peers, offering help and support willingly. The classroom became a haven where everyone felt heard and cared for.

However, as Mr. Williams stepped outside his classroom, the atmosphere changed. In the hallways, students hurriedly walked past each other without much interaction. Acts of kindness were sporadic and often overlooked. While Mr. Williams tried to promote kindness, the broader school community struggled to prioritize it. The absence of intentional acts of kindness left students longing for a more compassionate environment.

Inside Mr. Williams's classroom, the walls were adorned with educational posters, maps, and artwork created by his students. He carefully arranged the desks to facilitate collaboration and engagement. Soft, warm lighting created a comfortable ambiance, enhancing the learning experience. Students appreciated the thoughtful details, feeling a sense of belonging and pride in their classroom.

However, the aesthetics drastically changed as students entered other classrooms and the school corridors. Harsh fluorescent lights flickered above their heads, casting an uninviting glow. Uncomfortable, outdated seating arrangements hindered their ability to concentrate and engage fully. The physical environment lacked the attention to detail and aesthetic guidance Mr. Williams had cultivated in his classroom.

Mr. Williams's efforts to promote classroom support, school kindness, and aesthetic guidance were evident within the confines of his classroom. However, the broader school climate did not fully embody these elements. The absence of consistent acts of kindness and a lack of attention to aesthetic details throughout the school left a void in the students' experience, preventing them from reaping the full benefits of a positive school climate.

It became clear that promoting a positive school climate required collective efforts from all stakeholders. Mr. Williams continued to lead by example, hoping his dedication and unwavering commitment to classroom support, school kindness, and aesthetic guidance would inspire change beyond his classroom.

Discuss:

How does Mr. Williams effectively promote the elements of school climate, including classroom support, school kindness, and aesthetic guidance? How can his school community follow his example?

Ms. Jones

Ms. Jones stepped into her ninth-grade physics classroom at Newton High School, her eyes bright with enthusiasm. As her students filed in, she greeted each one with a warm smile and a genuine interest in their lives. She intently listened as they shared stories about their weekend adventures, showing empathy through her attentive body language and nodding along in understanding.

Throughout the class, Ms. Jones encouraged collaboration among her students. She skillfully facilitated group discussions, guiding them to work together to solve challenging physics problems. With a gentle tone and patient demeanor, she engaged with every question raised, ensuring that no student felt left behind. Her supportive approach built a sense of camaraderie among the students, fostering an environment where everyone felt comfortable sharing their ideas and helping one another.

Beyond the classroom walls, Ms. Jones took the time to make personal connections with her students. She celebrated their big and small achievements, acknowledging their hard work and dedication. When she noticed a student feeling down, she approached them with genuine concern, offering encouragement and reassurance. Her kindness was infectious, spreading a positive ripple effect throughout the classroom.

Inside her classroom, Ms. Jones transformed the learning space into an inviting oasis. Colorful posters adorned the walls, showcasing physics concepts and inspiring quotes. The desks were arranged in small clusters, which encouraged shared learning. Soft lighting bathed the room, casting a warm glow that fostered a calm and focused ambiance.

Despite Ms. Jones's efforts within her classroom, the wider school environment fell short in promoting kindness and embracing aesthetic guidance. The hallways lacked vibrant displays celebrating student achievements, and the lighting was harsh and impersonal. While present within Ms. Jones's realm, kindness did not consistently permeate the school culture, leaving untapped potential for fostering compassion and empathy among students.

Within her classroom, Ms. Jones succeeded in creating a positive school climate. Students felt supported, engaged, and inspired to learn. However, the school needed to embody the principles of school kindness and aesthetic guidance to realize a harmonious and uplifting learning environment.

Discuss:

How does Ms. Jones effectively promote the elements of school climate, including classroom support, school kindness, and aesthetic guidance? How can her school community follow her example?

Section 2C: Lesson Planning Activities

In chapters 1, 3, and 4 of this book, we are helping teachers implement principles of Transformational Education into *individual* lesson plans. However, in chapter 2, the principles are applied *school wide* and flow toward individual teachers, classrooms, and students. This section includes potential *school-wide initiatives* toward aesthetic guidance, school kindness, and classroom support rather than individual plans. The following are ideas for how individual teachers can implement micro-principles of school climate in individual classrooms.

Build Positive Relationships:
- Greet students individually by name every day.
- Have one-on-one conversations with students to learn about their interests and concerns.
- Attend school events outside of the classroom to support students' extracurricular activities.

Practice Empathy:
- Carefully listen when students share their thoughts, feelings, or problems.
- Acknowledge and validate students' emotions and experiences.
- Share personal stories or examples to connect with students on a deeper level.

Foster a Sense of Belonging:
- Incorporate icebreaker activities at the beginning of the school year to help students get to know each other.
- Create classroom norms that promote inclusivity and respect for all students.
- Display student work and achievements to celebrate their contributions.

Encourage Peer Support:
- Implement collaborative group projects where students work together to solve problems or complete tasks.

- Assign class buddies or mentors who can guide and support their peers.
- Encourage students to offer help or assistance to classmates who are struggling.

Use Positive Reinforcement:
- Give specific and meaningful praise to students when they demonstrate positive behaviors or make progress.
- Provide rewards or incentives for achieving academic goals or exhibiting desired behaviors.
- Create a "praise wall" where students can publicly acknowledge and appreciate each other's accomplishments.

Set Clear Expectations:
- Establish a set of classroom rules or expectations together with students to promote ownership and understanding.
- Communicate academic goals and performance criteria to guide students' efforts.
- Consistently enforce rules and expectations, applying fair and logical consequences when necessary.

Implement Cooperative Learning Activities:
- Assign group projects or presentations where students collaborate to complete a task.
- Use structured cooperative learning strategies like think-pair-share or jigsaw activities.
- Rotate group members regularly to provide opportunities for students to work with different peers.

Promote Student Voice and Choice:
- Hold regular class meetings where students can express their opinions and decide classroom matters.
- Provide students with options for choosing topics or projects that align with their interests.
- Encourage students to share their ideas and perspectives during class discussions or debates.

Provide Individual Support:
- Offer additional resources or materials to accommodate different learning styles or abilities.
- Provide extra guidance or scaffolding for students who require additional support.
- Collaborate with other specialists (e.g., special education teachers) to develop individualized learning plans.

Model Positive Behavior:
- Demonstrate active listening by maintaining eye contact and paraphrasing students' responses during discussions.
- Use respectful language and tone when addressing students and resolving conflicts.
- Show kindness and respect toward all students, modeling inclusive behavior.

The strategies below can help teachers implement the ideas effectively and create a supportive classroom environment for their students.

Strategies for Promoting Classroom Support:

Foster Inclusion and Acceptance:
- Incorporate diverse literature and resources that promote understanding and appreciation for different cultures and backgrounds.
- Organize cultural exchange events where students can share and learn about their traditions and customs.
- Assign group projects that require collaboration between students of different backgrounds or abilities.

Build Strong Relationships:
- Schedule regular class meetings or circles where students can express their thoughts and feelings in a supportive environment.
- Provide opportunities for students to work in pairs or small groups to develop trust and foster cooperation.
- Encourage students to listen and respond empathetically when their peers are sharing.

Create Peer Mentoring and Buddy Systems:
- Pair older students with younger ones to assist them with academic or social activities.

- Establish a peer support program where students can seek guidance or advice from their assigned mentors.
- Organize joint activities or projects that promote collaboration between older and younger students.

Recognize and Reward Kindness:
- Hold regular "Kindness Awards" ceremonies to acknowledge students who consistently demonstrate kind behavior.
- Create a "Kindness Wall" where students' acts of kindness are displayed, providing visible recognition to encourage others.
- Thank students who display kindness and highlight their actions during class discussions or assemblies.

Utilize Collaborative Projects:
- Assign group projects that require students to work together, share responsibilities, and support each other's ideas.
- Encourage students to help and assist their peers during group work or individual assignments.
- Reflect on the importance of teamwork and kindness in achieving shared goals during project debriefs.
- Provide Community Service and Outreach Opportunities:
- Organize a school-wide donation drive for a local charity or community organization.
- Arrange visits to nursing homes or hospitals where students can spend time with and bring joy to residents or patients.
- Engage students in environmental cleanup projects in the school or local neighborhood to promote community stewardship.

Strategies for Promoting Kindness:
Model Kindness:
- Greet students with a smile and using polite language.
- Show empathy and understanding when students face challenges.
- Resolve conflicts calmly and respectfully.

Teach Kindness:
- Read books or stories highlighting acts of kindness and discuss them with the students.

- Conduct class discussions on empathy and compassion, encouraging students to share their experiences.
- Use role-playing activities to practice responding with kindness in different situations.

Encourage Random Acts of Kindness:
- Create a kindness challenge board where students can write and share their acts of kindness.
- Assign each student a "kindness buddy" for whom they must perform a kind act each week.
- Brainstorm a list of random acts of kindness as a class and encourage students to choose and perform them independently.

Establish Kindness Challenges:
- Create a kindness bulletin board where students can post notes about acts of kindness they have witnessed or experienced.
- Implement a kindness jar, where students can write down the kind acts they observe or receive and read them aloud during class.

Strategies for Promoting Aesthetic Design:

Create a Thoughtful Classroom Design:
- Arrange desks in small groups or clusters to facilitate collaboration and communication.
- Use flexible seating options like bean bags, floor cushions, or standing desks to cater to different learning preferences.
- Create designated "creative corners" with art supplies, books, and comfortable seating for quiet reflection and creativity.

Incorporate Visual Arts:
- Display famous artworks or prints on the walls, discussing their significance and encouraging students to interpret them.
- Organize art appreciation lessons where students can create art pieces inspired by various styles and techniques.
- Host an art exhibition in the school to showcase students' artworks and celebrate their creativity.

Use Color Psychology:
- Paint one wall in a warm, inviting color like orange or yellow and another in a calming color like blue or green.

- Introduce colorful posters, charts, or educational materials that align with the subject being taught.
- Allow students to decorate their classroom folders or binders with their favorite colors to create a personal touch.

Enhance Lighting:
- Open curtains and blinds to let natural light in during the daytime, which positively impacts the mood and energy of the classroom.
- Use soft, adjustable desk lamps to provide focused lighting for individual or group work.
- Consider using color-changing LED lights to create a dynamic and visually appealing atmosphere during specific activities.

Appeal to Multiple Senses:
- Play instrumental music during independent work or reading time to set a relaxing ambiance.
- Introduce scented playdough or markers for sensory experiences during arts and crafts activities.
- Utilize tactile learning materials like textured cards or manipulatives for hands-on learning.

Utilize Nature and Greenery:
- Place potted plants or miniature indoor gardens around the classroom to add a touch of nature.
- Initiate a gardening project where students take care of plants and learn about the importance of nature.
- Create a nature-inspired reading nook with comfortable seating, plants, and nature-themed books.

Encourage Student Expression:
- Host regular poetry slams or creative writing competitions to showcase students' literary talents.
- Integrate music into lessons, allowing students to create songs related to their study topic.
- Organize an art club or extracurricular activity to explore various artistic mediums and styles.

Celebrate Diversity:
- Decorate the classroom with flags and cultural symbols representing the students' diverse backgrounds.
- Incorporate multicultural literature and stories that promote understanding and respect for different cultures.
- Arrange cultural events or presentations where students can share their traditions and customs.

Optimize Mindful Transitions:
- Create a rotating student-led art project for the hallway to keep it visually appealing and vibrant.
- Establish a "cleanup crew" of students responsible for keeping transitional spaces tidy and decorated with positive messages.
- Host a mural painting event involving students to beautify the school's transitional areas.

Model Aesthetic Awareness:
- Share personal experiences of art, music, or literature that have inspired you and impacted your life.
- Bring visually appealing items or artifacts to discuss during class, encouraging students to observe and appreciate them.
- Incorporate aesthetics into your teaching materials, presentations, and classroom displays to exemplify creativity and attention to detail.

The Transformational Education Application Guide *for Groups*

Sections 2D, 2E, 2F, 2G, and 2H are designed to serve *groups* for professional development, department collaboration, coaching, mentoring, or faculty and school-wide initiatives. These sections provide several applications and exercises to help teachers apply the principles of the TE model, which were introduced in the foundational book, *An Introduction to Transformational Education: Redefining Leadership in the Classroom*. These exercises are designed to enhance understanding, promote critical thinking, and provide practical examples for educators. These various applications and exercises in educational theory textbooks aim to bridge the gap between theory and practice, allowing teachers to actively engage with the content and apply it to their teaching contexts.

Section 2D: Reflection and Discussion

Group discussions promote collaboration and knowledge sharing among teachers. They provide opportunities for educators to discuss and debate educational theories, their applications, and their implications for teaching and learning. In this section, we will explore the qualities and practices of transformational educators and leadership, focusing on three key aspects: Classroom Support, School Kindness, and Aesthetic Guidance.

Instructions: In your group, take turns sharing your thoughts and experiences. Try to keep the discussion focused on the questions provided. Feel free to take notes during your discussion to share your insights with the larger group later.

Group Reflection Questions: Classroom Support
1. How can teachers cultivate empathy and care within the classroom environment to promote classroom support? What specific strategies or practices can they employ?
2. What role does peer support play in fostering classroom support? How can teachers and administrators encourage peer support among students?
3. How does classroom support contribute to student academic performance and socio-emotional health? Can you provide examples or evidence to support this connection?
4. How can teacher behaviors, such as meaning making and involving students in decision-making, enhance classroom support? How do these behav**iors contri**bute to the overall school climate?

Group Reflection Questions: School Kindness
1. How can teachers and administrators cultivate a culture of school kindness within the educational institution? What strategies or initiatives can be implemented to encourage intentional and voluntary acts of kindness?
2. How does school kindness contribute to students' socio-emotional well-being and overall life satisfaction? Can you provide examples or evidence to support this connection?

3. How can school kindness impact students' academic self-efficacy and engagement in their education? How does fostering a kind and supportive environment influence students' beliefs in their intellectual capacity and motivation?
4. What role does school kindness play in promoting prosocial behaviors and healthy interpersonal relationships among students, staff, and community members? How can schools create opportunities for students to engage in acts of kindness and encourage a culture of compassion and empathy?

Group Reflection Questions: Aesthetic Guidance
1. How can teachers and administrators create a favorable aesthetic experience within the classroom and school environment? What specific elements, such as lighting, seating arrangements, or visual displays, can contribute to a positive aesthetic impact on student learning and achievement?
2. In what ways can aesthetic guidance influence students' capacity for critical thinking and problem-solving? How does the physical presentation of the educational space contribute to students' ability to engage in creative problem-solving processes?
3. What are the four dimensions of aesthetic experience proposed by David Fenner? How can these dimensions be applied in designing and organizing classrooms and school spaces to enhance students' aesthetic experiences?
4. How does aesthetic guidance contribute to students' overall wellness and academic performance? Can you provide examples or evidence demonstrating the connection between positive aesthetic experiences and tangible student benefits?

Section 2E:
Peer Mentorship

Having a trusted member of the school community offer feedback provides valuable benefits. Their experienced perspective allows for objective observations and constructive criticism, enabling you and other stakeholders to gain insights into practices and areas for improvement.

Instructions: Have a community member, teacher, staff, or administration complete this school observation.

Classroom Support

- Teachers demonstrate understanding and share their students' feelings, creating a caring and supportive classroom environment.

Y / N | Comments: _____

_____

- All staff members, not just teachers, exhibit caring attitudes and behaviors toward students, fostering a positive atmosphere in the school community.

Y / N | Comments: _____

_____

- Students show support and care for one another, promoting community and belonging within the classroom.

Y / N | Comments: _____

_____

- Teachers engage in activities that help students connect and find relevance in their learning, enhancing their sense of community and motivation.

Y / N | Comments: _____

_____

- Students are given opportunities to participate in decision-making processes within the classroom, making them feel valued and essential to their education.

Y / N | Comments: _____

_____

- A structured system is in place to encourage peer support among students, promoting connectedness to school and fostering socio-emotional well-being.

Y / N | Comments: _____

_____

- Educators actively strategize and create conditions that support social-emotional learning (SEL), recognizing its importance in student development and success.

  Y / N | Comments: _____

- Student voices and experiences are highlighted and shared, demonstrating the positive impact of classroom support on their well-being and academic performance.

  Y / N | Comments: _____

- The school acknowledges the significance of classroom support as a determining factor in the overall school climate and recognizes the role of teacher behaviors in shaping student outcomes.

  Y / N | Comments: _____

- The school community actively seeks and incorporates evidence-based strategies and approaches to enhance classroom support and promote student success in various areas, including academic performance, socio-emotional health, and future career paths.

  Y / N | Comments: _____

School Kindness
- School personnel demonstrate kindness in interactions with students, colleagues, and parents.

  Y / N | Comments: _____

- The curriculum includes lessons and activities that promote kindness and its impact on individuals and the community.

Y / N | Comments: _____

_____

- An inclusive environment is encouraged where all students feel valued and respected.

Y / N | Comments: _____

_____

- Acts of kindness through verbal praise, certificates, or small tokens of appreciation are recognized and celebrated.

Y / N | Comments: _____

_____

- There are opportunities for older students to mentor and support younger students.

Y / N | Comments: _____

_____

- Students are involved in volunteering and fundraising activities to help others.

Y / N | Comments: _____

_____

- Conflicts and behavioral issues are addressed through dialogue and teaching opportunities, focusing on empathy and problem-solving.

Y / N | Comments: _____

_____

- Regular acts of kindness are encouraged through challenges, campaigns, or bulletin boards.

Y / N | Comments: _____

_____

- Resources and support systems are provided for students' emotional well-being.

Y / N | Comments: _____

_____

- Training opportunities are offered for teachers to promote kindness and empathy.

Y / N | Comments: _____

_____

Aesthetic Guidance
- The physical spaces within the school direct students' attention in ways that promote positive outcomes and resolutions.

Y / N | Comments: _____

_____

- The classrooms and school spaces create a sense of order, structure, and purpose.

Y / N | Comments: _____

_____

- Visual cues and elements guide students' attention toward learning and growth.

Y / N | Comments: _____

_____

- The school spaces provide opportunities for students to make choices and exercise autonomy.

Y / N | Comments: _____
_____

- Students are encouraged to express their individuality and preferences within the classroom environment.

Y / N | Comments: _____
_____

- Students feel empowered and supported in making decisions related to their learning and engagement.

Y / N | Comments: _____
_____

- The school spaces are designed to create a safe and emotionally supportive student environment.

Y / N | Comments: _____
_____

- The physical elements help students gain emotional distance from sources of fear or oppression.

Y / N | Comments: _____
_____

- Strategies are in place to address and alleviate stress, anxiety, or negative emotions within the school climate.

Y / N | Comments: _____
_____

- The classrooms and school spaces encourage students to explore, discover, and make new connections.

Y / N | Comments: _____
_____

Section 2F: Scenario

This section presents a specific teaching scenario and asks teachers to apply the theories and strategies they have learned to address the challenges or opportunities presented. They encourage teachers to think critically, make informed decisions, and consider the practical implications of the theories.

Instructions: Read the following hypothetical scenario that teachers may encounter in their classrooms. Utilize the discussion questions to analyze the situation, identify challenges, and propose solutions based on the theories and concepts discussed in the textbook.

Scenario

In the suburbs of Greater Philadelphia, there stood a remarkable school called Harmony Heights Academy. At the heart of this institution was a visionary school leader named Mrs. Rodriguez, who believed wholeheartedly in the importance of classroom support, school kindness, and aesthetic guidance to create an exceptional learning environment for her students.

In the classrooms of Harmony Heights Academy, teachers, staff, and students formed a tight-knit community. Mrs. Rodriguez encouraged her teachers to exhibit empathetic and caring behaviors, creating a culture of support that extended to every student. For instance, teachers offered one-on-one support and extra resources when a student faced difficulties with a particular subject. This classroom support improved academic performance and nurtured a sense of belonging and camaraderie among the students.

Mrs. Rodriguez's commitment to school kindness extended beyond the classroom walls. The school actively promoted acts of kindness throughout the campus. They organized monthly kindness challenges, encouraging students to act compassionately and write about their experiences. The school's kindness also included involving students in community service projects, fostering a sense of responsibility and empathy for others.

Yet Mrs. Rodriguez knew that a truly transformative educational experience involved more than just emotions and actions; it also required attention to the physical environment. She took great care in ensuring that the school's aesthetics significantly inspired creativity and a love for learning. Colorful murals adorned the hallways, reflecting the diverse backgrounds of the student body and fostering a sense of pride in their heritage. The classrooms were designed to be comfortable and inviting, with flexible seating arrangements that allowed for collaborative learning experiences.

As the years passed, the impact of Mrs. Rodriguez's leadership and her commitment to the three pillars of school climate became evident. Harmony Heights Academy became known as a place where students excelled academically and grew into compassionate and confident individuals. Testimonials from students and parents alike praised the caring teachers, the culture of kindness, and the visually stimulating learning spaces.

The reputation of Harmony Heights Academy spread far and wide. The school was known as an educational gem. Families from all corners of the region sought admission for their children, eager to be a part of the school's transformative journey. Mrs. Rodriguez's approach, based on research and proven leadership principles, had turned Harmony Heights Academy into a beacon of education.

The legacy of Mrs. Rodriguez and Harmony Heights Academy continued to shine as the years passed. The school's commitment to classroom support, school kindness, and aesthetic guidance continued to impact the lives of countless students who had the privilege of being part of this extraordinary learning community. At the center of it all was a school leader who believed in the power of kindness, support, and beauty to create a world of possibilities for her beloved students.

Group Discussion:
In the fictional scenario of Harmony Heights Academy, we witnessed how the three elements of classroom support, school kindness, and aesthetic guidance combined to create a transformative school climate. As educators and administrators, we understand the importance of nurturing a positive and inclusive learning environment for our students. Reflecting on your content area, grade level, and school culture, explore how you can apply these elements to foster a truly exceptional educational experience.

Classroom Support:
- How can we enhance classroom support across all grade levels and subject areas?
- What strategies can teachers employ to provide individual support to struggling students?
- How can we encourage peer support and collaboration among students to strengthen the sense of community in classrooms?
- How can we promote empathy and understanding among teachers, staff, and students?

School Kindness:
- How can we encourage and recognize acts of kindness among students, staff, and the school community?
- What initiatives can we implement to promote school-wide community service and foster a sense of responsibility and empathy for others?
- How can we ensure that acts of kindness become integral to the school culture rather than isolated events?

- What role can administrators play in modeling and promoting kindness throughout the school?

Aesthetic Guidance:
- How can we improve the physical environment of our school to make it more visually stimulating and conducive to learning?
- What aspects of the school's aesthetics can we modify or enhance to reflect the diverse backgrounds and cultures of our students?
- How can teachers incorporate aesthetic elements into their classrooms to inspire creativity and critical thinking among students?
- What role can students play in contributing to the aesthetics of their learning spaces?

Synergy and Collaboration:
- How can we ensure that classroom support, school kindness, and aesthetic guidance synergize to create a transformative school climate?
- How can administrators and teachers collaborate to integrate these elements into the school's mission and vision?
- How can we measure and assess the impact of these initiatives on student well-being, academic performance, and overall school climate?
- How can we involve parents and the broader school community in supporting and reinforcing these elements?

As educators and administrators, we can shape the school climate and create an environment where students thrive academically, emotionally, and socially. By embracing classroom support, school kindness, and aesthetic guidance school wide, we can pave the way for a transformative educational experience that leaves a lasting positive impact on the lives of our students. Let's explore practical strategies and collaborative efforts to make our school a haven of learning, compassion, and creativity.

Section 2G: Role-Playing

Role-Playing Exercises:

Role-playing activities allow teachers to simulate instructional scenarios or interactions with students. Use the following role-playing exercises to assist you in exploring different teaching approaches, experimenting with strategies, and gaining insights into the practical applications of educational theories.

Role-Play 1

Title: Advice from a Veteran Educator

Objective: The five-minute role-play exercise aims to provide Mr. Lamb, a first-year teacher, with practical insights from Mrs. Rivera, a seasoned teacher, on creating a positive and supportive classroom environment using the elements of classroom support, school kindness, and aesthetic guidance.

Roles:
- Mrs. Rivera: The seasoned teacher who shares her experiences and tips.
- Mr. Lamb: The first-year teacher seeking guidance on classroom climate.

Instructions:

Setting the Scene:
- The role-play is set in the teachers' lounge during a break period.
- Mr. Lamb approaches Mrs. Rivera, seeking advice on improving the classroom climate.

Role-Play Process:

Step 1: Mr. Lamb's Concerns
- Mr. Lamb expresses his concerns about the classroom atmosphere and student engagement.
- He mentions that he is unsure how to create a positive and supportive environment for his students.

Step 2: Mrs. Rivera's Insights
- Mrs. Rivera listens attentively and reassures Mr. Lamb that it's normal to feel uncertain in the first year of teaching.
- She explains that building a positive classroom climate involves three key elements: classroom support, school kindness, and aesthetic guidance.

Step 3: Classroom Support
- Mrs. Rivera advises Mr. Lamb to show empathy and care toward his students.
- She suggests using positive reinforcement and praising students' efforts and achievements.
- Mrs. Rivera recommends incorporating mindfulness or relaxation exercises to reduce stress and improve well-being.

Step 4: School Kindness
- Mrs. Rivera emphasizes the importance of creating a kind and respectful classroom community.
- She encourages Mr. Lamb to promote kindness among students and acknowledge and appreciate their positive behaviors.
- Mrs. Rivera suggests involving students in group activities that foster teamwork and cooperation.

Step 5: Aesthetic Guidance
- Mrs. Rivera explains that the physical environment can impact student learning and emotions.
- She suggests organizing the classroom in a way that encourages collaboration and creativity.
- Mrs. Rivera recommends using colorful visuals and displays to make the classroom visually appealing and inviting.

Debrief and Reflection:
- After the role-play, Mrs. Rivera and Mr. Lamb briefly discuss the importance of each element in creating a positive classroom climate.
- Mrs. Rivera assures Mr. Lamb that it takes time and practice to implement these strategies effectively.

Action Plan:
- Mrs. Rivera advises Mr. Lamb to start with small changes and gradually incorporate these elements into his classroom routine.
- She encourages him to reflect on the impact of these changes and adapt them to suit the needs of his students.

Support and Encouragement:
- Mrs. Rivera offers ongoing support and tells Mr. Lamb that he can always reach out for guidance or share his experiences with her.
- Mr. Lamb expresses gratitude for Mrs. Rivera's advice and feels more confident about creating a positive classroom climate.

Note: The five-minute role-play exercise is a condensed version of the longer role-play, focusing on creating a positive classroom climate. It aims to provide Mr. Lamb with practical insights and encouragement from Mrs. Rivera, helping him feel more confident in his teaching journey.

Role-Play 2

Title: Promoting School Kindness

Objective: The five-minute role-play exercise aims to showcase how a seasoned teacher, Mrs. Litner, presents a school kindness initiative to the school administrator, Mr. Anderson, to promote a culture of kindness and respect school wide.

Roles:
- Mrs. Litner: The seasoned teacher advocating for the school kindness initiative.
- Mr. Anderson: The school administrator open to discussions and improvements.

Instructions:

Setting the Scene:
- The role-play is set in Mr. Anderson's office during a scheduled meeting.
- Mrs. Litner has requested this meeting to discuss her school kindness initiative proposal.

Role-Play Process:

Step 1: Mrs. Litner's Introduction
- Mrs. Litner begins the conversation by expressing her gratitude for the meeting and dedication to creating a positive and caring school environment.
- She introduces the concept of the school kindness initiative and its potential impact on students' well-being and overall school climate.

Step 2: Presenting the School Kindness Initiative
- Mrs. Litner explains that the school kindness initiative aims to foster a culture of kindness and respect.
- She proposes a school-wide campaign that promotes and recognizes acts of kindness among students, staff, and faculty.

Step 3: Key Components of the Initiative
- Mrs. Litner suggests organizing regular kindness challenges or events to encourage students to engage in acts of kindness toward one another.

- She proposes creating a "Kindness Wall" in a prominent area where students and staff can share stories of kindness they have witnessed or experienced.
- Mrs. Litner recommends implementing kindness lessons and activities in the curriculum to emphasize the value of kindness and empathy.

Administrator's Response:
- Mr. Anderson listens attentively to Mrs. Litner's proposal and supports the school's kindness initiative.
- He acknowledges the importance of promoting a positive school climate and commends Mrs. Litner for her dedication.

Collaborative Planning:
- Mrs. Litner and Mr. Anderson brainstorm ways to involve the entire school community in the initiative.
- They discuss integrating the kindness campaign into school events, assemblies, and extracurricular activities.

Commitment and Next Steps:
- Mr. Anderson expresses his commitment to implementing the school kindness initiative.
- They agree to form a committee of teachers, staff, and student representatives to plan and execute the initiative.
- Mrs. Litner and Mr. Anderson set a follow-up meeting to review the progress and make any necessary adjustments.

Note: The five-minute role-play exercise focuses solely on a school kindness initiative. The exercise highlights the importance of promoting kindness and respect within the school community, encouraging collaboration and planning between the seasoned teacher and the school administrator. The role-play emphasizes creating a positive and caring school climate by implementing the school kindness initiative.

Role-Play 3

Title: Addressing Financial Matters

Introduction: The upcoming role-play exercise will simulate a conversation between a school board financial gatekeeper and a school president. This exercise aims to provide participants with an example of effective communication when discussing financial matters.

One of the most challenging tasks for school leaders is justifying budget allocations, particularly for initiatives that may seem nonessential to financial gatekeepers but are vital to students' overall well-being and performance. In this role-play, the school president will discuss allocating funds toward "aesthetic guidance," a concept that may initially seem less straightforward in its impact on student outcomes.

As you will see, the school president leverages research and existing models to support their points and articulates how aesthetic guidance can contribute to tangible benefits for the students. They also respond to all questions and concerns the financial gatekeeper raises, aiming to find common ground and consensus.

We hope this role-play will serve as a valuable demonstration of how you can effectively communicate the need for specific budget allocations to financial gatekeepers. Adopting a similar approach can help ensure that crucial aspects of education, like aesthetic guidance, receive the financial support they require.

School Board Financial Gatekeeper (SBFG): Good morning, President. As we look into the upcoming fiscal year, there have been discussions about allocating funds toward certain initiatives. Specifically, I'd like to understand more about the value of giving funds to what you term "aesthetic guidance." Could you explain this concept a bit more?

School President (SP): Absolutely, I'd be glad to. When we talk about aesthetic guidance, we refer to the efforts put into creating an educational space that is appealing to the senses and conducive to learning. It's about creating an environment where students feel engaged, inspired, and free to explore. This means not just making the school visually pleasing but fostering a physical space to enhance the learning experience.

SBFG: Interesting. However, our focus has always been on academics. Why should we invest in the aesthetics of the school space?

SP: While academics is crucial, it's not the only element contributing to a student's educational experience. The physical aspect of the school space forms one-third of what we call the "school climate." Research shows that aesthetic experiences can profoundly impact students, improving their capacity to think critically and creatively, enhancing their learning behavior, and even boosting academic achievement.

SBFG: That sounds promising, but how exactly does aesthetic guidance work? What are the elements that we need to consider?

SP: We work with four dimensions based on David Fenner's theory of aesthetic experience. These include "object directness," where the school environment directs positive attention; "felt freedom," where the space enables students to make choices freely; "detached affect," where the environment helps students emotionally detach from fear or oppression; and "active discovery," where the space encourages students to discover new connections and solve problems creatively.

SBFG: How can we ensure that our investments in aesthetic guidance will have a tangible, positive impact on our students?

SP: Our approach to aesthetic guidance is based on well-established research and tested leadership theory, and we already see its impact in our daily school life. For instance, we've noted improvements in student wellness and performance. It's not about creating a "pretty school" but cultivating an environment that promotes learning, creativity, and freedom. By investing in this, we're investing in a holistic education for our students. A well-designed and engaging environment is integral to our Transformational Education model, as we've experienced here at The Lincoln Center.

SBFG: I see your point, President. This could be a transformative direction for our school and significantly impact our students' learning experiences. Let's work together to detail the steps for implementing this initiative and determine how best to allocate our resources.

SP: I'm pleased to hear that, and I look forward to partnering with you on this important initiative. I believe that this investment in aesthetic guidance will enhance our school climate and lead to a noticeable improvement in student engagement and achievement.

Note: This role-play demonstrates effective communication when discussing the allocation of funds toward "aesthetic guidance" in a school setting. The school president highlights the impact of aesthetics on student outcomes, supports their points with research, and addresses concerns raised by the financial gatekeeper. The conversation concludes with an agreement to collaborate on implementing the initiative. Participants can advocate for necessary educational budget allocations by adopting a similar approach.

Role-Play 4

Title: Addressing Financial Matters

Introduction: This role-playing exercise illustrates a hypothetical conversation between a school administrator, Mr. Santos, and the school board president, Ms. Jackson. It provides valuable insights into how educational professionals can approach financial gatekeepers when advocating for certain budget allocations.

The crux of the conversation centers around the concept of "school kindness"—the intentional behaviors that benefit students, driven not by external rewards or punishments but from the genuine desire to uplift and support one another. It explores how such an abstract, often overlooked concept can be tied to tangible outcomes like socio-emotional well-being, academic self-efficacy, prosocial behaviors, and increased engagement.

The dialogue showcases how Mr. Santos marshals the evidence from research to make a compelling case for investing in school kindness initiatives, highlighting their value for the immediate school climate and broader academic performance and student life satisfaction.

This role-playing exercise is a practical tool to guide attendees in shaping persuasive arguments when engaging with financial decision-makers. By focusing on an initiative's direct and indirect benefits and quantifying or qualifying its impacts, you can effectively bridge the gap between a novel idea and its potential for tangible, positive outcomes. This approach can be beneficial in many contexts, where the value of an investment may not be immediately obvious but has significant long-term potential.

Ms. Jackson: Mr. Santos, we're discussing the school budget, and, as you know, we need to be strategic with our funds. I've heard you talking about the importance of school kindness. Could you elaborate on how it adds value to our school?

Mr. Santos: Absolutely, Ms. Jackson. When we talk about school kindness, we mean those intentional actions that benefit another person, motivated not by rewards or punishments but by the genuine intention to help. This is a critical part of our Transformational Education model.

Ms. Jackson: How does this relate to our students' socio-emotional well-being and academic performance? We need to make sure our investment has a tangible impact.

Mr. Santos: Research has shown that school kindness is linked to students' socio-emotional well-being, which addresses their emotional health within their social environment. When we intentionally choose to benefit our students, it improves their social wellness.

Ms. Jackson: Can you explain how this translates to an improved academic environment?

Mr. Santos: Yes, of course. School kindness positively affects students' life satisfaction and their belief in their academic ability. This belief, or self-efficacy, involves confidence in their motivation, behaviors, and social skills to succeed academically. In other words, by fostering a kind environment, we're cultivating a better space for learning and growth.

Ms. Jackson: So you suggest that kindness contributes to better interpersonal relationships and academic engagement?

Mr. Santos: Precisely. School kindness helps students enact prosocial behaviors—cooperation, helping, sharing, and giving—leading to healthier interpersonal relationships. The result? An increase in students' cognitive, behavioral, and emotional engagement in their education.

Ms. Jackson: Interesting. What role does school kindness play within the Transformational Education model?

Mr. Santos: Given the results of various studies on classroom support and other caring behaviors, we position school kindness in a moderating role within the Transformational Education model. We believe that school kindness can catalyze more kindness between students, staff, and community members, ultimately leading to a more constructive and nurturing environment.

Ms. Jackson: So by investing in initiatives that promote school kindness, we're creating a better climate for our students and potentially enhancing their academic performance.

Mr. Santos: Exactly, Ms. Jackson. It invests in our students' holistic growth and creates a school environment where everyone thrives.

Note: This role-play emphasized the value of advocating for budget allocations by linking abstract concepts, like school kindness, to tangible outcomes. Mr. Santos effectively demonstrated the importance of investing in initiatives that promote school kindness by presenting research evidence and quantifying the impacts. The exercise highlighted the significance of considering immediate and long-term benefits, even when not immediately apparent. It underscored the power of creating a nurturing environment for holistic student growth and academic success.

Section 2H:
Interdisciplinary and Collaborative Lesson Planning

The following may be used by school departments, by faculty, or for school-wide initiatives. These activities guide teachers in designing lesson plans using the theories and strategies discussed in the textbook. They may involve creating objectives, selecting appropriate instructional methods, developing assessment strategies, and adapting content for diverse learners.

Lesson Plans

Note: In chapters 1, 3, and 4, of this book, we are helping teachers implement principles of Transformational Education into *individual* lesson plans. However, in chapter 2, the principles are applied school wide and flow toward individual teachers, classrooms, and students. Below are potential *comprehensive initiatives* toward aesthetic guidance, school kindness, and classroom support rather than individual plans.

Improvement Plan Proposal for Forestville High School:

Improve Classroom Support:
- Teacher Training: Encourage teachers to adopt empathetic and caring behaviors toward their students. Provide training in empathy and emotional intelligence.
- Peer Support Program: Develop a peer support program where students are trained to support each other academically and emotionally. This can also involve establishing a mentoring program between older and younger students.
- Inclusive Decision-Making: Involve students in classroom decision-making processes to foster a sense of ownership and community.

Classroom Support Initiatives
- Implement a Mentoring Program: Establish a system where every student has a designated staff member as a mentor whom they can turn to for support and advice.
- Develop Student Support Groups: These groups can be facilitated by trained staff to encourage students to share their experiences and provide support for each other.
- Build Student-Teacher Dialogue: Foster a two-way dialogue between teachers and students where students can share their concerns or suggestions about classroom dynamics or teaching methods.
- Class Reflection Time: Allocate time in the classroom for collective reflection and discussion on what is working well and what needs improvement.
- Enhance Classroom Physical Environment: Make classrooms more learner friendly and comfortable to encourage better concentration and participation.
- Integrate Socio-Emotional Learning: Incorporate social-emotional learning (SEL) into the curriculum to foster self-awareness, self-management, responsible decision-making, relationship skills, and social awareness.

- Interactive Learning: Encourage collaborative learning through group work, project-based learning, and interactive discussions to promote peer support and cooperation.
- Regular Feedback Mechanism: Develop a system for students to give and receive regular, constructive feedback on their work and behavior.
- Learning Differentiation: Cater to different learning styles and speeds using various teaching methods and resources.
- Personal Development Plans: Create individual learning plans to cater to each student's needs, promoting a sense of ownership of their learning process.

Foster School Kindness:
- Kindness Programs: Create initiatives that encourage and reward acts of kindness within the school community. For instance, a "Kindness Week" where students and staff perform random acts of kindness.
- Mental Health Education: Integrate socio-emotional learning in the curriculum to promote students' mental health. Provide regular workshops on topics such as empathy, kindness, and compassion.
- Cultivate Positive Relationships: Encourage healthy interpersonal relationships through teamwork, collaboration, and conflict resolution training.

School Kindness Initiatives
- Encourage Random Acts of Kindness: Create a culture that appreciates and celebrates acts of kindness, no matter how small.
- Peer Mentoring Program: Encourage older students to mentor younger ones, promoting empathy and understanding.
- Kindness Curriculum: Incorporate kindness into the curriculum, making it part of daily lessons and activities.
- Kindness Recognition: Regularly recognize and reward acts of kindness through a recognition system.
- School-Wide Kindness Challenges: Organize regular school-wide challenges that promote acts of kindness and community service.
- Kindness Clubs: Create student-led clubs that plan and implement kindness initiatives.

- Collaboration with Local Community: Organize joint kindness initiatives with the local community, promoting a sense of shared responsibility.
- Staff Modeling: Encourage staff to model kind behavior, showing students how to act kindly in different situations.
- Kindness in School Policies: Incorporate kindness into school policies and procedures, showing that it's a core value of the school.
- Empathy Training: Provide training for both staff and students to develop their empathy skills.

Enhance Aesthetic Guidance:
- Optimize Physical Environment: Improve the physical learning environment to boost learning and engagement. This can include strategic seating arrangements, good lighting, stimulating colors, and inviting decorations.
- Art and Culture Integration: Incorporate art and culture into the curriculum to improve aesthetic appreciation. Regularly change wall displays to feature student artwork, cultural artifacts, or educational content.
- School Beautification Projects: Engage students in projects that improve the school's aesthetics, such as a school garden or mural. This promotes creativity, teamwork, and pride in the school environment.

Aesthetic Guidance Initiatives
- Classroom Redesign: Make classrooms more conducive to learning by adding more natural light, comfortable seating, and interactive learning spaces.
- School Beautification Projects: Encourage students to participate in beautifying the school through art projects or gardening.
- Display Student Work: Regularly display student work around the school to instill a sense of pride and ownership.
- Create Learning Zones: Create different learning zones within the school, like quiet study areas, interactive zones, and reading corners.
- Environmental Considerations: Implement green initiatives within the school, such as recycling programs and energy-saving measures.

- Outdoor Learning Spaces: Develop outdoor classrooms or learning spaces to enhance students' connection with nature.
- Art and Music: Incorporate art and music into the everyday life of the school, not just as extracurricular activities.
- Sensory Spaces: Develop sensory spaces for students who need time to self-regulate and calm down.
- Accessible Design: Make sure all spaces are accessible and inclusive for students of all abilities.
- Involve Students in Design: Involve students in designing their learning spaces, giving them a sense of ownership and control.

Achieving these goals requires continuous efforts, investment, and monitoring. Evaluating the progress and effectiveness of these strategies will involve regular surveys of student wellness, academic performance, and perception of school climate. Hopefully, this approach will create a nurturing and productive environment at Forestville High School, thereby improving student well-being and academic performance.

Chapter 3

Promoting Student Wellness

This chapter contains several exercises and applications to help teachers apply the theoretical content found in chapter 3 of the accompanying foundational text, *An Introduction to Transformational Education*. These exercises are designed to enhance understanding, promote critical thinking, and provide practical examples for educators. These various applications and exercises in educational theory textbooks aim to bridge the gap between theory and practice, allowing teachers to actively engage with the content and apply it to their teaching contexts.

- **Section 3A: Self-Assessment and Reflection**
- **Section 3B: Case Studies**
- **Section 3C: Lesson Planning Activities**
- **Section 3D: Reflection and Discussion**
- **Section 3E: Peer Mentorship**
- **Section 3F: Scenarios**
- **Section 3G: Role-Playing**
- **Section 3H: Interdisciplinary and Collaborative Lesson Planning**

Section 3A:
Self-Assessment and Reflection

The Student Wellness Self-Assessment is a tool that allows educators to evaluate the promotion of student wellness in their school context. This activity provides self-assessment prompts to help teachers reflect on their instructional practices, beliefs, and professional growth. It will encourage educators to evaluate their strengths, identify improvement areas, and set further development goals. **This self-assessment consists of three sections: Connectedness, Self-Efficacy, and Socio-Emotional Well-Being.** Each section contains a series of statements related to the respective category.

Student Wellness Self-Assessment

Instructions: For each statement, indicate your agreement level or practice frequency.

5—Strongly Agree, 4—Agree, 3—Neutral, 2—Disagree, 1—Strongly Disagree

Connectedness

Connectedness refers to how students feel part of the community within their school context, family, and friends. Connectedness comprises students' internal experiences, perceptions, and feelings about school. These encompass important notions that include a sense of belonging, relationships with staff and other students, and the feeling that learning is a priority.

_____ 1. I prioritize creating a sense of belonging in my classroom.

_____ 2. I actively build relationships with my students and encourage positive relationships among students.

_____ 3. I foster a supportive and inclusive classroom environment where students feel valued and respected.

_____ 4. I promote student engagement and participation in class activities.

_____ 5. I provide personalized academic assistance and socio-emotional support to my students.

_____ 6. I establish connections between classroom learning and the broader school community.

_____ 7. I encourage and facilitate adult mentoring opportunities for students with teachers, counselors, and staff members.

_____ 8. I support students during transitions, particularly between primary and secondary school.

_____ 9. I am knowledgeable about research studies and best practices for fostering student connectedness.

_____ 10. I actively reflect on my teaching practices and seek opportunities for improvement in fostering connectedness.

Connectedness Total Score _____ /50

Self-Efficacy

Self-efficacy is the component of student wellness, which measures students' belief that they can be successful when carrying out a particular task. In education, self-efficacy surrounds students' ability to control their academic activities. Self-efficacy refers to the degree to which students sense the power to make choices that impact themselves and their larger contexts.

_____ 1. I consistently provide specific and constructive feedback to my students to help them believe in their ability to complete tasks such as writing essays or solving math problems.

_____ 2. I regularly give my students opportunities to make choices in the classroom, such as selecting topics for projects or deciding on group work strategies, to empower them to control their academic activities.

_____ 3. I explicitly teach my students strategies for managing their time and resources effectively, helping them develop a sense of control over their academic activities.

_____ 4. I design engaging activities and lesson plans that require active participation and critical thinking, promoting cognitive engagement in the classroom.

_____ 5. I firmly believe that students' self-efficacy levels significantly impact their achievement more than their previous academic accomplishments.

_____ 6. I actively stay informed about research and studies on self-efficacy and its influence on academic performance.

_____ 7. I demonstrate Transformational Leadership behaviors by providing mentorship, guidance, and inspiration to my students, positively influencing their self-efficacy.

_____ 8. I create a supportive and nurturing classroom environment where struggling students feel comfortable seeking help and successful students feel encouraged to continue challenging themselves.

_____ 9. I recognize that my behaviors as a teacher can impact student self-efficacy in various subjects or extracurricular activities, such as supporting students' belief in their abilities in science experiments or language learning.

_____ 10. I intentionally incorporate activities and discussions that foster self-reflection and a growth mindset, knowing that developing self-efficacy will positively impact my students' academic performance.

    Self-Efficacy Total Score _____/50

Socio-Emotional Well-Being

Socio-Emotional Well-Being refers to students' initiation, cultivation, and response to others, which all move them to form relationships with peers, school staff, parents, and relatives. Socio-Emotional health represents a student's belief in self, belief in others, emotional competence, and engaged living. The school setting fosters essential abilities such as cooperation, following directions, demonstrating self-control, and paying attention through socio-emotional skills. In addition, socio-emotional development involves trust, confidence, pride, friendship, affection, and humor.

_____ 1. I regularly engage in activities that promote positive relationships among students, such as group projects, collaborative discussions, and team-building exercises.

_____ 2. I provide specific and constructive feedback to students, reinforcing their belief in their abilities and encouraging a growth mindset.

_____ 3. I teach and model emotional regulation strategies, such as deep breathing or mindfulness exercises, to help students develop and enhance their emotional competence.

_____ 4. I create a classroom environment that is welcoming, inclusive, and respectful, where students feel safe to express themselves and take risks.

_____ 5. I incorporate cooperative learning structures like group work and peer teaching to encourage students to develop cooperation and teamwork skills.

_____ 6. I actively listen to my students and show empathy and understanding when addressing their socio-emotional needs and concerns.

_____ 7. I implement consistent behavior management strategies that promote self-control and provide clear expectations for paying attention during classroom activities.

_____ 8. I regularly use formative assessments, surveys, or check-ins to assess and monitor students' socio-emotional well-being.

_____ 9. I prioritize building trust and positive relationships with my students, encouraging open communication, and promoting pride and belonging within the classroom community.

_____ 10. I seek professional development opportunities, read relevant research and literature, and actively engage in self-reflection to enhance my knowledge and skills in supporting students' socio-emotional well-being.

Socio-Emotional Well-Being Total Score _____/50

Interpretation of Scores by Section:

Scoring:
- Add up your scores for all the statements.
- The higher the total score, the more you practice the target teacher behavior in the classroom.

Interpretation:
- 41–50: You effectively incorporate the target teacher behavior strategies in your classroom.
- 31–40: Your use of the target teacher behavior in the classroom is moderate. Continue to build on your current strategies to enhance this behavior.
- 21–30: You have some level of the target teacher behavior in your classroom, but there is room for improvement.
- 10–20: Your use of the target teacher behavior in the classroom may be limited.

Note: This self-assessment tool is designed to indicate your current use of the Transformational Education target for the classroom or school context. It is not a comprehensive evaluation and should be used as a starting point for reflection and professional growth.

Individual Reflection Questions
Transformational Education and Student Wellness

These questions encourage teachers to reflect on their teaching practices, beliefs, and experiences. They help educators connect theory to their instructional context and promote self-reflection and professional growth.

Instructions: Utilize the following questions to reflect on your current practices regarding student wellness discussed in chapter 3 of *An Introduction to Transformational Education*. You are encouraged to write your thoughts down for later reflection and discussion with a mentor.

1. How do teacher behaviors contribute to the transformation of students' educational experience? How can these behaviors be fostered and encouraged in the classroom?
2. What is the role of student wellness in the relationship between teacher behaviors and student performance outcomes? How can educators promote student wellness in their teaching practices?
3. In what ways does a sense of connectedness impact students' overall academic performance and well-being? How can educators create a supportive and inclusive school community that enhances students' sense of connectedness?
4. How does self-efficacy influence students' engagement and academic performance? What strategies can educators employ to enhance students' self-efficacy in their academic pursuits?
5. What is the significance of socio-emotional well-being in students' development and academic achievement? How can educators integrate socio-emotional skills into their teaching practices to support students' well-being?
6. How can teacher-student relationships and positive classroom environments contribute to the development of socio-emotional skills in students? What specific approaches can educators use to build these relationships and create positive learning environments?
7. Reflecting on the Transformational Education model, how can you incorporate the concepts of connectedness, self-efficacy, and socio-emotional well-being into your teaching practices to promote positive student outcomes?

8. Are there any specific research studies or interventions mentioned in the text that you find particularly interesting or relevant to your teaching context? How might you apply their findings in your classroom?
9. How can you involve students in their wellness and development? What strategies or activities can empower students to take ownership of their academic success and well-being?
10. How can you collaborate with other educators, administrators, and support staff to create a holistic approach to student wellness and promote a positive school culture?

Section 3B: Case Studies

Case studies present real or hypothetical scenarios teachers may encounter in their classrooms. They require educators to analyze the situation, identify challenges, and propose solutions based on the theories and concepts discussed in the textbook.

Instructions: Read the provided case studies carefully. Take note of the critical points and details presented in the text. Aim to arrive at well-rounded and thoughtful answers that consider various perspectives. Refer to the case study as needed to support your responses.

To benefit from the case study of Mr. Patel and understand his employment of or failure to employ crucial teacher behaviors, analyze Mr. Patel's ability to foster connectedness, self-efficacy, and socio-emotional well-being.

Mr. Patel

Mr. Patel stepped into his bustling classroom, a genuine smile lighting up his face. He weaved through the desks, pausing to exchange warm greetings with each student, their eyes brightening with a sense of belonging. The room hummed with animated conversations as classmates connected, sharing laughter and ideas.

As the lesson began, Mr. Patel posed a challenging math problem, his voice filled with encouragement. John, hunched over his desk, hesitated to join the discussion. Sensing his unease, Mr. Patel knelt beside him, offering gentle guidance and reassurance. Slowly, John's confidence blossomed, his eyes gleaming with newfound self-belief.

During a lesson, Sarah's face grew clouded with worry. Sensing her distress, Mr. Patel paused, his voice filled with empathy. "It's okay, Sarah. I understand how you feel," he said softly, his eyes conveying a genuine concern. He shared anecdotes of his struggles, validating her emotions and fostering a sense of trust. Sarah's anxious expression gradually melted away, replaced by a glimmer of hope.

Months passed, and Mr. Patel's commitment to student wellness deepened. He dedicated time for one-on-one check-ins, sitting across from students, their voices echoing with hopes and dreams. He tailored his teaching methods, presenting concepts in diverse ways, igniting sparks of understanding, and empowering students to take charge of their learning.

Mr. Patel organized team-building activities outside the classroom, unleashing a cascade of laughter and camaraderie. His students connected on a deeper level, forming bonds that transcended the boundaries of the math classroom. The once-shy John now laughed freely among friends, his voice no longer muffled by self-doubt.

Through his unwavering dedication, Mr. Patel transformed his classroom into a sanctuary of connectedness, self-efficacy, and socio-emotional well-being. Within those walls, students flourished, their hearts filled with a sense of belonging, their minds brimming with confidence. As they embarked on their educational journey, Mr. Patel's impact radiated, nurturing the seeds of student wellness that would bloom long after the final bell had rung.

Discuss:

In reflecting on Mr. Patel's teaching practices, share examples of how he effectively promotes student connectedness, self-efficacy, and socio-emotional well-being in his classroom. Additionally, identify instances where Mr. Patel falls short in addressing these elements and suggest alternative strategies he could employ to improve student wellness.

Ms. Chen

Ms. Chen entered her vibrant classroom, her warm smile radiating a sense of belonging. As she moved among the students, her genuine interest in their lives shone through in her conversations. A chorus of laughter and friendly banter filled the air, weaving an intricate web of connectedness.

Ms. Chen's attentive gaze swept the room during class discussions, lingering on Lily at the back. Lily's hesitant posture spoke volumes of her isolation. Sensing her need for connection, Ms. Chen approached Lily, engaging her in one-on-one conversations and encouraging her to share her insights. Slowly but surely, Lily's guarded demeanor softened, and a flicker of belonging emerged in her eyes.

Ms. Chen assigned a creative writing project to nurture self-efficacy that challenged her students to explore their voices. She provided personalized feedback, highlighting their unique strengths and talents. As she handed Michael's paper back, her eyes sparkled with admiration. "Your storytelling ability is truly remarkable," she said, genuine enthusiasm coloring her words. Michael's chest swelled with pride, his belief in his potential growing stronger.

Throughout the year, Ms. Chen wove socio-emotional well-being threads into her classroom's fabric. Inspirational quotes adorned the walls, evoking a sense of calm and encouragement.

During vulnerable moments, Ms. Chen shared her experiences, allowing her students to see her as more than just a teacher. She created a safe space for open discussions about emotions and mental health, fostering empathy and understanding among her students.

One day, Emily approached Ms. Chen with tears streaming down her face, her anxiety overwhelming her. Ms. Chen gently pulled up a chair, offering a comforting presence. With unwavering compassion, she listened intently, validating Emily's emotions without judgment. She shared coping strategies and recommended resources, providing a lifeline of support. As Emily left her office, a glimmer of hope danced in her eyes, and her spirits lifted.

As the year ended, Ms. Chen marveled at the transformation within her classroom. Students collaborated with enthusiasm, their voices intertwining in harmonious discussions. The air buzzed with creative energy as they confidently shared their written masterpieces. Kindness and understanding became the norm, fostering an atmosphere of support and empathy.

Ms. Chen's classroom had become a sanctuary of connectedness, self-efficacy, and socio-emotional well-being. Through her genuine connections, personalized encouragement, and compassionate support, she had nurtured a community where students blossomed into confident individuals, ready to face the world armed with resilience, empathy, and a deep belief in their worth.

Discuss:

In reflecting on Ms. Chen's teaching practices, share examples of how she effectively promotes student connectedness, self-efficacy, and socio-emotional well-being in her classroom. Additionally, identify instances where Ms. Chen falls short in addressing these elements and suggest alternative strategies she could employ to improve student wellness.

Section 3C:
Lesson Planning Activities

These activities guide teachers in designing lesson plans using the theories and strategies discussed in the textbook. They may involve creating objectives, selecting appropriate instructional methods, developing assessment strategies, and adapting content for diverse learners.

Instructions: Use the following examples to guide you in your lesson planning.

Example 1

Grade Level: 9th Grade

Subject: Science

Lesson Title: Exploring Ecosystems: Interactions and Sustainability

Duration: 60 minutes

Objective:
- Students will understand the concept of ecosystems, their components, and their interactions.
- Students will analyze the interrelationships within ecosystems, including food chains, energy flow, and nutrient cycling.
- Students will evaluate the impact of human activities on ecosystem health and discuss strategies for sustainability.

Instructional Methods:
- Whole-Class Discussion: Engage students in a discussion about ecosystems, defining key terms such as biotic and abiotic factors, producers, consumers, decomposers, and trophic levels.
- Interactive Lecture: Present information about different types of ecosystems (e.g., forests, deserts, aquatic ecosystems) and discuss their unique characteristics and adaptations.
- Group Work: Divide students into small groups and assign each group a specific ecosystem to research and present to the class, highlighting its components and interrelationships.
- Hands-On Activities: Conduct laboratory experiments or simulations to demonstrate concepts such as energy transfer through food chains and the cycling of nutrients in ecosystems.
- Multimedia Resources: Show videos, interactive websites, or virtual reality experiences to represent diverse ecosystems and their dynamics visually.

Assessment Strategies:
- Formative Assessment: Monitor students' participation and engagement during class discussions and group work activities.

- Group Presentation: Evaluate each group's presentation on their assigned ecosystem, assessing their understanding of ecosystem components, interactions, and adaptations.
- Laboratory Report: Have students write a report summarizing their observations and findings from the hands-on activities, focusing on the energy flow and nutrient cycling within an ecosystem.
- Case Study Analysis: Provide a case study scenario related to ecosystem degradation caused by human activities and ask students to analyze the impact of these activities on the ecosystem and propose strategies for sustainability.

Adapting Content for Diverse Learners:
- Visual Learners: Provide visual aids, diagrams, and charts to illustrate the components, interactions, and processes within ecosystems.
- Auditory Learners: Include audio recordings or presentations with clear explanations of scientific concepts and encourage class discussions to enhance understanding.
- Kinesthetic Learners: Incorporate hands-on activities such as role-playing, ecosystem simulations, or creating models to allow students to engage in experiential learning.
- English Language Learners: Offer bilingual resources, simplified language, and opportunities for peer collaboration to support comprehension and language acquisition.
- Students with Special Needs: Provide additional support, such as visual prompts, simplified instructions, or assistive technology, to accommodate individual learning needs.

Note: By focusing on the scientific concepts surrounding ecosystems and incorporating principles of student wellness into the lesson plan design, this lesson aims to promote a holistic understanding of ecological principles while nurturing student engagement, collaboration, and diverse learning styles.

Example 2

Grade Level: 11th Grade

Subject: English Language

Lesson Title: Exploring *Macbeth*: Analyzing Themes and Character Development

Duration: 60 minutes

Objective:
- Students will analyze the themes and character development in Shakespeare's play *Macbeth*.
- Students will critically evaluate the impact of the characters' choices and actions on the overall plot.
- Students will apply principles of empathy and self-reflection to understand the psychological aspects of the characters.

Instructional Methods:
- Whole-Class Discussion: Engage students in a discussion about the themes in *Macbeth*, such as ambition, guilt, fate, and the corrupting influence of power.
- Close Reading: Assign specific scenes or soliloquies to students and have them analyze the language, imagery, and symbolism used by Shakespeare to convey character motivations and themes.
- Group Activities: Divide students into small groups and assign each group a specific character from *Macbeth*. Have them explore the character's development throughout the play, focusing on critical choices and actions.
- Role-Play: Organize a dramatic enactment of selected scenes, allowing students to embody the characters and gain a deeper understanding of their motivations and emotions.
- Creative Writing: Assign students a reflective writing task where they analyze a character's perspective or inner thoughts, encouraging empathy and self-reflection.

Assessment Strategies:
- Formative Assessment: Observe students' participation and engagement during class discussions and group activities, focusing on their ability to analyze themes and character development.
- Group Presentation: Evaluate each group's presentation on their assigned character, assessing their understanding of the character's development, motivations, and impact on the plot.
- Written Analysis: Have students write an analytical essay discussing the choices and actions of a character in *Macbeth* and their consequences on the overall storyline and themes.
- Reflection Writing: Assess students' reflective writing pieces, evaluating their ability to empathize with the characters and provide thoughtful insights into their psychological complexities.

Adapting Content for Diverse Learners:
- Visual Learners: Incorporate visual aids such as character maps, timelines, and visual representations of key scenes to enhance comprehension and analysis.
- Auditory Learners: Utilize audio recordings of key scenes or soliloquies, class discussions, and group activities that encourage verbal expression and critical thinking.
- Kinesthetic Learners: Engage students in role-playing activities, allowing them to physically embody the characters and interact with the text on a deeper level.
- English Language Learners: Provide bilingual resources, simplified language versions of the play, and opportunities for peer collaboration to support comprehension and language acquisition.
- Students with Special Needs: Offer additional support, such as graphic organizers, guided prompts, or modified assignments, based on individual learning needs and accommodations.

Note: By analyzing *Macbeth*'s themes and character development while incorporating principles of empathy and self-reflection, this lesson aims to foster a deeper understanding of Shakespeare's play and its relevance to the human condition. Students will engage in critical thinking, collaboration, and various learning styles, allowing for a comprehensive exploration of the text's literary elements and psychological complexities.

Example 3

Grade Level: 7th Grade

Subject: History

Lesson Title: The War of 1812: Exploring Causes, Consequences, and Historical Perspectives

Duration: 60 minutes

Objective:
- Students will examine the causes and consequences of the War of 1812.
- Students will analyze different historical perspectives surrounding the conflict.
- Students will apply critical thinking and empathy to understand the impact of the war on the various groups involved.

Instructional Methods:
- Whole-Class Discussion: Engage students in a discussion about the reasons behind the War of 1812, such as impressment, maritime trade disputes, and conflicts with Native American tribes.
- Document Analysis: Provide primary and secondary sources of the war, including letters, speeches, maps, and illustrations. Have students analyze these sources to identify different perspectives and motivations of key figures and groups.
- Role-Play: Assign students different roles, such as American soldiers, British officials, Native American leaders, or American citizens, and conduct a mock debate where students defend their perspectives on the war.
- Group Research Projects: Divide students into small groups and assign each group a specific aspect of the war, such as major battles, key figures, or the impact on indigenous peoples. Students will research and present their findings to the class, discussing multiple perspectives.
- Creative Projects: Encourage students to create artwork, write historical fiction narratives, or produce short films depicting individuals' or groups' experiences and viewpoints during the War of 1812.

Assessment Strategies:
- Formative Assessment: Monitor students' participation and engagement during class discussions, document analysis, and role-play activities.
- Group Presentation: Evaluate each group's presentation on their assigned topic, assessing their ability to analyze different perspectives, present accurate information, and engage the class.
- Written Reflection: Assign students a reflective writing task where they discuss the causes, consequences, and perspectives of the War of 1812, emphasizing critical thinking and empathy.
- Creative Project Assessment: Evaluate students' creative projects based on their ability to incorporate historical accuracy, multiple perspectives, and the impact of the war on various groups.

Adapting Content for Diverse Learners:
- Visual Learners: Utilize visual aids such as maps, illustrations, and infographics to enhance understanding of historical events and perspectives.
- Auditory Learners: Incorporate audio recordings of historical speeches or dramatic readings of primary source documents to engage students' listening skills.
- Kinesthetic Learners: Organize hands-on activities, such as mock debates, role-plays, or the creation of artifacts related to the war, to actively involve students in the learning process.
- English Language Learners: Provide bilingual resources, simplified language versions of texts, and opportunities for peer collaboration to support comprehension and language acquisition.
- Students with Special Needs: Offer additional support, such as guided prompts, graphic organizers, or modified assignments, based on individual learning needs and accommodations.

Note: By examining the causes, consequences, and historical perspectives of the War of 1812 while applying principles of critical thinking and empathy, this lesson aims to foster a comprehensive understanding of the conflict and its impact. Students will engage in active learning, collaboration, and diverse learning styles, enabling them to analyze historical events from multiple angles and develop a nuanced understanding of the complexities of the war.

Example 4

Grade Level: 10th Grade

Subject: Health

Lesson Title: The Dangers of Smoking: Understanding the Health Consequences and Promoting Healthy Choices

Duration: 60 minutes

Objective:
- Students will understand the health risks associated with smoking and tobacco use.
- Students will analyze the factors that contribute to smoking initiation and addiction.
- Students will apply principles of decision-making and personal responsibility to promote healthy choices regarding tobacco use.

Instructional Methods:
- Whole-Class Discussion: Engage students about the health consequences of smoking, such as lung cancer, heart disease, respiratory issues, and the dangers of secondhand smoke.
- Multimedia Presentation: Show videos, images, and testimonials that illustrate the physical and social impacts of smoking on individuals and communities.
- Case Studies: Present real-life scenarios where smoking-related decisions and addiction play a role. Ask students to analyze the factors that influenced those decisions and discuss potential strategies for prevention and cessation.
- Group Research Projects: Divide students into small groups and assign each group a specific aspect of smoking, such as the chemical composition of tobacco, advertising tactics, or the influence of peer pressure. Students will research and present their findings, emphasizing the need for informed decision-making.
- Personal Reflection: Assign students a reflective writing task where they discuss their thoughts and feelings about smoking, including their perceptions, influences, and personal commitments to staying smoke free.

Assessment Strategies:
- Formative Assessment: Monitor students' participation and engagement during class discussions, multimedia presentations, and group activities.
- Group Presentation: Evaluate each group's presentation on their assigned aspect of smoking, assessing their ability to convey accurate information, engage the class, and promote awareness of the health risks.
- Written Reflection: Assess students' reflective writing pieces, evaluating their ability to express their thoughts, analyze influences, and commit to healthy choices.
- Peer Assessment: Incorporate peer evaluations or group discussions where students provide feedback and constructive suggestions to their classmates' presentations and reflections.

Adapting Content for Diverse Learners:
- Visual Learners: Utilize visual aids such as infographics, charts, and diagrams to present statistical data, facts, and comparisons of smoking and its health consequences.
- Auditory Learners: Include audio recordings or interviews with individuals affected by smoking-related illnesses to engage students' listening skills and emotional connections.
- Kinesthetic Learners: Facilitate hands-on activities such as interactive games or role-plays to simulate the physical and social impacts of smoking, emphasizing experiential learning.
- English Language Learners: Provide bilingual resources, simplified language versions of texts, and opportunities for peer collaboration to support comprehension and language acquisition.
- Students with Special Needs: Offer additional support, such as visual prompts, simplified instructions, or modified assignments, based on individual learning needs and accommodations.

Note: By exploring the health risks of smoking while applying principles of decision-making and personal responsibility, this lesson aims to raise awareness among students about the dangers of tobacco use and empower them to make informed choices regarding their health. Students will engage in critical thinking, research, reflection, and diverse learning styles, fostering a deeper understanding of the impact of smoking on individual well-being and public health.

Lesson Plan Template

Grade Level: [7th–12th Grade]

Subject: [Subject/Discipline]

Lesson Title: [Lesson Topic]: Applying Student Wellness in [Subject/Discipline]

Duration: [Duration of the Lesson]

Objective:
- Students will understand the [Subject/Discipline] concept/content.
- Students will analyze the relevance of student wellness principles to the [Subject/Discipline] topic.
- Students will apply principles of student wellness to enhance learning and promote overall well-being.

Instructional Methods:
- Whole-Class Discussion: Engage students in a discussion about the core concepts/content of [Subject/Discipline] and introduce the principles of student wellness.
- Active Learning Activities: Incorporate hands-on activities, group work, or simulations that require students to actively participate and apply their understanding of the subject while considering student wellness principles.
- Reflection and Self-Assessment: Provide opportunities for students to reflect on their learning experiences, assess their well-being, and identify self-care and academic growth strategies.
- Authentic Connections: Establish connections between the subject matter and students' personal lives, interests, and goals to enhance engagement and relevance.
- Differentiated Instruction: Adapt instructional strategies and materials to accommodate diverse learners and address the various components of student wellness.

Assessment Strategies:
- Formative Assessment: Observe students' active participation, engagement, and application of student wellness principles during class activities and discussions.

- Performance Tasks: Assign tasks or projects that require students to demonstrate their understanding of the subject while incorporating student wellness principles.
- Self-Assessment: Provide self-assessment tools or reflection prompts for students to evaluate their well-being, progress, and the effectiveness of applying student wellness principles in their learning process.
- Peer Assessment: Encourage students to provide constructive feedback and support their peers in practicing student wellness principles.
- Summative Assessment: Evaluate students' overall understanding of the subject and their ability to connect it with student wellness principles through exams, essays, or presentations.

Adapting Content for Diverse Learners:
- Visual Learners: Utilize visual aids, diagrams, charts, or infographics to enhance understanding and illustrate connections between the subject and student wellness principles.
- Auditory Learners: Incorporate audio recordings, oral presentations, or discussions to engage students' listening skills and facilitate comprehension.
- Kinesthetic Learners: Include hands-on activities, simulations, or movement-based tasks that allow students to engage physically with the subject while considering student wellness principles.
- English Language Learners: Provide bilingual resources, simplified language versions of texts, and opportunities for peer collaboration to support comprehension and language acquisition.
- Students with Special Needs: Offer additional support, accommodations, and modified assignments based on individual learning needs to ensure access to the subject matter and student wellness principles.

Note: By incorporating the principles of student wellness into [Subject/Discipline] lessons, this template aims to create a learning environment that promotes academic understanding and supports students' overall well-being. Students will engage in active learning, reflection, and applying student wellness principles, fostering a holistic approach to their education.

The Transformational Education Application Guide *for Groups*

Sections 3D, 3E, 3F, and 3G are designed to serve *groups* for professional development, department collaboration, coaching, mentoring, or faculty and school-wide initiatives. These sections provide several applications and exercises to help teachers apply the principles of the TE model, which were introduced in the foundational book, *An Introduction to Transformational Education: Redefining Leadership in the Classroom*. These exercises are designed to enhance understanding, promote critical thinking, and provide practical examples for educators. These various applications and exercises in educational theory textbooks aim to bridge the gap between theory and practice, allowing teachers to actively engage with the content and apply it to their teaching contexts.

Section 3D:
Reflection and Discussion

Group discussions promote collaboration and knowledge sharing among teachers. They provide opportunities for educators to discuss and debate educational theories, their applications, and their implications for teaching and learning. This section will explore transformational educators' and leadership qualities and practices, focusing on three key aspects: Connectedness, Self-Efficacy, and Socio-Emotional Well-Being.

Instructions: In your group, take turns sharing your thoughts and experiences. Try to keep the discussion focused on the questions provided. Feel free to take notes during your discussion to share your insights with the larger group later.

Group Reflection Questions: Connectedness
- In what ways can teacher behaviors promote a sense of connectedness in students? How do these behaviors impact students' engagement, motivation, and achievement?
- Reflecting on your teaching practices, how do you promote connectedness in your classroom/school? What strategies have you found effective in fostering a sense of belonging and strong relationships among students?
- How can schools and educators collaborate to create a supportive and inclusive environment that enhances connectedness for all students, particularly those who may feel marginalized or isolated?
- Based on your understanding of the importance of connectedness, how might you modify your teaching approaches or strategies to further prioritize and strengthen this component of student wellness in your educational setting?

Group Reflection Questions: Self-Efficacy
- Reflect on when you witnessed a student displaying high self-efficacy in their academic activities. What factors contributed to their belief in their ability to succeed?
- Share an experience where you observed a student lacking self-efficacy in a particular task or subject. What strategies did you employ to help them build confidence and improve their belief in their abilities?

- Think about your teaching practices. In what ways do you currently promote self-efficacy among your students? Are there any specific strategies or approaches you use to help students develop a sense of control over their academic activities?
- Consider the concept of "choice" mentioned in the text. How can you incorporate more opportunities for student choice in your classroom to enhance their sense of self-efficacy? Share any examples or ideas you have in mind.
- How might promoting self-efficacy in one subject or activity (e.g., math class, robotics club, Spanish class, soccer team) spill over into other areas of a student's academic and personal life? Share any experiences or insights you have regarding the wide-ranging impact of self-efficacy.

Group Reflection Questions: Socio-Emotional Well-Being
- Reflect on your teaching practices. How do you currently promote socio-emotional well-being in your classroom? Are there specific strategies or activities you implement to foster students' belief in self, belief in others, emotional competence, and engaged living?
- Based on the text, socio-emotional skills can be learned. How can you create a supportive and caring teacher-student relationship that builds connectedness? What specific actions or behaviors can you incorporate to foster a positive classroom environment for socio-emotional development?
- Socio-emotional well-being elements such as trust, confidence, pride, friendship, affection, and humor contribute to students' sense of connection and safety. Reflect on your classroom environment. How can you enhance these elements to create a more inclusive and supportive space for all students?
- The text mentions that interventions to build socio-emotional skills have been associated with improved attitudes, behavior, and academic achievement. Can you recall any experiences where you witnessed these positive outcomes due to focusing on socio-emotional well-being? Share specific examples and reflect on the impact it had on the students.

- As educators, how can we collaborate and support each other in promoting socio-emotional well-being in our respective classrooms? Share ideas and suggestions for creating a supportive network to learn from one another and collectively enhance student wellness.

Section 3E:
Peer Mentorship

Having a trusted mentor observe your classroom and offer feedback provides valuable benefits. Their experienced perspective allows for objective observations and constructive criticism, enabling you to gain insights into your teaching practices and areas for improvement. Their guidance helps refine instructional strategies, enhance student engagement, and address specific challenges.

Instructions: Use this one-to-one observation tool with a colleague or mentor to boost your professional growth, expand your teaching repertoire, and foster self-reflection.

Connectedness

- The teacher uses literature, videos, or visual aids with diverse characters.

Y / N | Comments: _____

_____

- The teacher intervenes when students engage in disrespectful behavior, addressing the issue.

Y / N | Comments: _____

_____

- During class discussions, the teacher ensures that every student has an opportunity to express their ideas and actively listens to each contribution.

Y / N | Comments: _____

_____

- The teacher praises and acknowledges students for their strengths, talents, or ideas.

Y / N | Comments: _____

_____

- The teacher encourages students to share personal experiences or cultural backgrounds, fostering an appreciation for diversity.

Y / N | Comments: _____

_____

- The teacher engages in one-on-one conversations with students, asking open-ended questions about their hobbies, passions, or academic goals.

Y / N | Comments: _____

_____

- The teacher takes notes or keeps a record of students' interests and abilities to inform their instructional approach and provide personalized support.

Y / N | Comments: _____

- The teacher offers additional assistance or guidance to students who require extra help, either during or outside of class hours.

Y / N | Comments: _____

- The teacher adapts instructional materials or assignments to meet individual students' specific needs or learning styles.

Y / N | Comments: _____

- The teacher uses strategies like think-pair-share or class discussions to foster student engagement and interaction.

Y / N | Comments: _____

Self-Efficacy
- The teacher regularly gives students opportunities to make choices in the classroom, such as selecting topics for projects or deciding on group work strategies, to empower them to control their academic activities.

Y / N | Comments: _____

- The teacher explicitly teaches students strategies for managing their time and resources effectively, helping them develop a sense of control over their academic activities.

Y / N | Comments: _____

- The teacher designs engaging activities and lesson plans that require active participation and critical thinking, promoting cognitive engagement in the classroom.

Y / N | Comments: _____

_____

- The teacher strongly believes that students' self-efficacy levels significantly impact their achievement more than their previous academic accomplishments.

Y / N | Comments: _____

_____

- The teacher actively stays informed about research and studies on self-efficacy and its influence on academic performance.

Y / N | Comments: _____

_____

- The teacher demonstrates Transformational Leadership behaviors by providing students mentorship, guidance, and inspiration, positively influencing their self-efficacy levels.

Y / N | Comments: _____

_____

- The teacher creates a supportive and nurturing classroom environment where struggling students feel comfortable seeking help and successful students feel encouraged to continue challenging themselves.

Y / N | Comments: _____

_____

- The teacher recognizes that their behaviors can impact student self-efficacy in various subjects or extracurricular activities, such as supporting students' belief in their abilities in science experiments or language learning.

Y / N | Comments: _____

_____

- The teacher intentionally incorporates activities and discussions that foster self-reflection and a growth mindset, knowing that developing self-efficacy will positively impact students' academic performance.

Y / N | Comments: _____

_____

Socio-Emotional Well-Being
- The teacher regularly engages in activities that promote positive relationships among students, such as group projects, collaborative discussions, and team-building exercises.

Y / N | Comments: _____

_____

- The teacher provides specific and constructive feedback to students, reinforcing their belief in their abilities and encouraging a growth mindset.

Y / N | Comments: _____

_____

- The teacher teaches and models emotional regulation strategies, such as deep breathing or mindfulness exercises, to help students develop and enhance their emotional competence.

Y / N | Comments: _____

_____

- The teacher creates a classroom environment that is welcoming, inclusive, and respectful, where students feel safe to express themselves and take risks.

Y / N | Comments: _____

_____

- The teacher incorporates cooperative learning structures, such as group work and peer teaching, to encourage students to develop cooperation and teamwork skills.

Y / N | Comments: _____

_____

- The teacher actively listens to their students and shows empathy and understanding when addressing their socio-emotional needs and concerns.

Y / N | Comments: _____

_____

- The teacher implements consistent behavior management strategies that promote self-control and provide clear expectations for paying attention during classroom activities.

Y / N | Comments: _____

_____

- The teacher regularly uses formative assessments, surveys, or check-ins to assess and monitor students' socio-emotional well-being.

Y / N | Comments: _____

_____

- The teacher prioritizes building trust and positive relationships with their students, encouraging open communication, and promoting pride and belonging within the classroom community.

Y / N | Comments: _____

_____

- The teacher seeks professional development opportunities, reads relevant research and literature, and actively engages in self-reflection to enhance their knowledge and skills in supporting students' socio-emotional well-being.

Y / N | Comments: _____
_____

Section 3F: Scenarios

This section presents a specific teaching scenario and asks teachers to apply the theories and strategies they have learned to address the challenges or opportunities presented. They encourage teachers to think critically, make informed decisions, and consider the practical implications of the theories.

Instructions: Read the following hypothetical scenario that teachers may encounter in their classrooms. Utilize the discussion questions to analyze the situation, identify challenges, and propose solutions based on the theories and concepts discussed in the textbook.

Scenario 1

As Jenna entered Ms. Watterson's math class, she couldn't help but feel a sense of belonging. The classroom walls were adorned with colorful posters showcasing the achievements of previous students, creating an atmosphere of celebration and inclusion. Ms. Watterson greeted each student with a warm smile and took the time to engage in genuine conversations, learning about their interests and goals.

Jenna noticed that Ms. Watterson intentionally mixed students of different abilities during group activities, encouraging collaboration and teamwork. The class became a vibrant community where ideas were shared freely and everyone felt valued. Ms. Watterson fostered an environment where mistakes were celebrated as learning opportunities, creating a safe space for students to take risks and explore new concepts.

Jenna thrived in this connected classroom. She eagerly participated in discussions, feeling comfortable sharing her perspectives and seeking clarification when needed. Her classmates became study partners and friends, supporting and encouraging each other's growth. Ms. Watterson's attentive mentoring significantly impacted Jenna's academic journey, as she saw herself as part of a larger community invested in her success.

Omar, on the other hand, found it challenging to connect with his classmates. As an introverted student, he often felt overwhelmed in social settings. Recognizing this, Ms. Watterson implemented icebreaker activities and collaborative projects that gradually broke Omar's barriers. She paired him with supportive and empathetic classmates who helped him feel more at ease.

But where Omar truly thrived was in his growing self-efficacy. Ms. Watterson consistently recognized his efforts and highlighted his unique strengths. When presenting challenging problems, she encouraged Omar to take the lead, allowing him to demonstrate his abilities and make decisions about problem-solving strategies. With each successful solution, Omar's confidence grew, and he began to embrace the belief that he could excel in math.

However, in the absence of explicit discussions about socio-emotional well-being, some aspects were left unaddressed in Ms. Watterson's class. While the focus on academic achievement and skill development was apparent, the classroom lacked deliberate activities and conversations that nurtured emotional competence and empathy. Students like Jenna and Omar received substantial support in their connectedness and self-efficacy, but their emotional well-being needed more attention.

Reflecting on her teaching practices, Ms. Watterson recognized the importance of integrating socio-emotional learning principles into her math class. She sought resources and professional development opportunities to enhance her understanding of fostering her students' emotional intelligence, empathy, and overall well-being. With a renewed focus on holistic student development, Ms. Watterson began incorporating activities encouraging self-reflection, emotional expression, and supportive peer interactions.

By infusing socio-emotional well-being principles into her math class, Ms. Watterson created a more balanced and enriching educational experience for her students. She realized that addressing students' emotional and social needs alongside academic growth was crucial in shaping well-rounded individuals ready to navigate the world's challenges beyond the classroom.

Group Discussion:

Using the following, discuss the above scenario considering the student wellness principles:

1. Based on the scenario presented, how does Ms. Watterson foster a sense of connectedness in her math class? How do her actions align with the concept of connectedness described in the textbook? Identify any challenges or opportunities related to connectedness in the scenario.

2. Reflecting on the scenario, discuss the impact of self-efficacy on student performance and academic engagement. How does Ms. Watterson promote self-efficacy in her math class, and how does it positively influence student learning? Identify any potential challenges or areas for improvement in fostering self-efficacy.

3. In the context of socio-emotional well-being, analyze the strengths and weaknesses of Ms. Watterson's math class. How does the scenario demonstrate the importance of socio-emotional skills in a classroom environment? Identify any missed opportunities or challenges in addressing socio-emotional well-being in the scenario.

4. Drawing on the theories and concepts discussed in the textbook, propose specific strategies or interventions that Ms. Watterson could implement to enhance connectedness among all students, including those struggling with social interactions. How might these strategies address the challenges or opportunities identified in the scenario?

5. Consider the role of socio-emotional learning in fostering a balanced educational experience. Based on the scenario, discuss practical implications and specific actions Ms. Watterson could take to integrate socio-emotional learning principles into her math class. How might addressing socio-emotional well-being benefit students' overall academic performance and well-being?

Scenario 2

Sylvana walked into Mr. Urban's Intro to Psychology class, excited and nervous. As she found a seat, Mr. Urban stood at the front of the classroom, radiating warmth and enthusiasm. He greeted each student individually, making eye contact and offering encouraging words. Sylvana felt a sense of comfort in Mr. Urban's presence, sensing that he genuinely cared about his students' well-being.

Throughout the semester, Mr. Urban skillfully integrated socio-emotional well-being into the class. He started each session with a mindfulness exercise, guiding the students in deep breathing and reflective moments. The classroom atmosphere became a sanctuary where students could temporarily let go of their outside worries and focus on their inner selves. Sylvana appreciated these moments of calm and found herself feeling more grounded and centered.

Mr. Urban's teaching style was inclusive and compassionate, recognizing that students' emotions played a vital role in their academic journey. He regularly incorporated discussions about emotions, mental health, and personal growth into his lessons. He encouraged students to share their experiences, fostering a sense of trust and vulnerability within the class. Sylvana found solace in these discussions, realizing she was not alone in her struggles.

Pedro, an ambitious and determined student, thrived under Mr. Urban's guidance in terms of self-efficacy. Mr. Urban recognized Pedro's potential and consistently challenged him with complex assignments and thought-provoking questions. Whenever Pedro faced difficulties, Mr. Urban provided constructive feedback and reassurance, instilling a belief in Pedro's ability to overcome obstacles. Pedro's confidence soared as he tackled challenging tasks and achieved impressive results.

However, while Mr. Urban excelled in socio-emotional well-being and self-efficacy, he struggled with connectedness. Though he encouraged open discussions, Sylvana noticed that the class lacked opportunities for students to form deep connections with one another. Group work was limited, and few activities fostered collaboration and interaction. Sylvana longed for more chances to connect with her classmates, share ideas, and learn from one another.

As the semester progressed, Sylvana and Pedro admired Mr. Urban's dedication to their socio-emotional well-being and his ability to nurture their self-efficacy. They valued his empathy, the mindfulness exercises, and his unwavering support. However, they couldn't help but feel that the class lacked a stronger sense of connectedness. They yearned for more collaborative projects, team-building activities, and opportunities to develop peer relationships.

Recognizing the importance of connectedness, Sylvana approached Mr. Urban after class one day and shared her thoughts. Mr. Urban listened attentively, acknowledging the gap in his teaching approach. He realized the value of fostering a stronger sense of community within the classroom and appreciated Sylvana's input. Determined to address this concern, Mr. Urban began brainstorming ways to integrate more interactive and collaborative activities into future lessons, ensuring that students would have more opportunities to connect and learn from one another.

As the semester came to a close, Sylvana and Pedro reflected on their experiences in Mr. Urban's class. They appreciated his commitment to their socio-emotional well-being and the belief he instilled in their self-efficacy. While the class lacked connectedness initially, they admired Mr. Urban's openness to feedback and his willingness to adapt his teaching practices. Sylvana and Pedro left the class grateful for their support and hoped that future students would benefit from an even stronger sense of connectedness in Mr. Urban's classroom.

Group Discussion:
Using the following, discuss the above scenario in light of student wellness principles:

1. Considering the scenario presented, how would you apply the principles of connectedness to Mr. Urban's Intro to Psychology class to foster a stronger sense of community among the students? What strategies or activities would you implement to encourage student collaboration and interaction?

2. Reflecting on the strengths demonstrated in socio-emotional well-being within Mr. Urban's class, how could you further enhance the integration of socio-emotional learning into your classroom? Share specific strategies or approaches you would use to support students' emotional competence, empathy, and overall well-being.

3. In relation to self-efficacy, discuss how you would empower your students to take control of their learning and foster a belief in their abilities. Share specific practices or techniques you would implement to help students develop a growth mindset and actively engage in their academic journey.

4. Analyze the potential consequences of the weak aspect of connectedness in Mr. Urban's class. How might the lack of opportunities for students to form deep connections with their peers impact their overall learning experience and well-being? Propose specific steps or activities to address this challenge and create a more connected classroom environment.

5. Reflecting on the principles of student wellness discussed in the scenario, examine the interplay between connectedness, self-efficacy, and socio-emotional well-being. How do these components interact and support one another in fostering positive student outcomes? Share practical strategies or approaches that you would adopt to create a holistic and supportive classroom environment that addresses all three aspects of student wellness.

Section 3G: Role-Playing

Role-Playing Exercises:

Role-playing activities allow teachers to simulate instructional scenarios or interactions with students. Use the following role-playing exercises to assist you in exploring different teaching approaches, experimenting with strategies, and gaining insights into the practical applications of educational theories.

Role-Play 1

Title: A Guidance Counselor Explains Self-Efficacy

Objective: The five-minute role-play aims to provide Shanika, a ninth-grade student, with an understanding of self-efficacy. Her guidance counselor, Ms. Kohl, kindly explains the concept and offers practical tips on how to apply it.

Roles:
- Shanika: a ninth-grade student
- Ms. Kohl: the school guidance counselor

Instructions:

Setting the Scene:
- Shanika knocks on the door and enters Ms. Kohl's office.

Role-Play Process:
- Shanika: Hi, Ms. Kohl. Can I talk to you for a moment?
- Ms. Kohl: Of course, Shanika. Please, have a seat. What's on your mind?
- Shanika: Well, I've struggled to understand the content in Mr. Miller's chemistry class. Everything he teaches goes over my head, and I'm losing confidence in my abilities.
- Ms. Kohl: I'm sorry to hear that, Shanika. It can be frustrating when you're having trouble grasping a subject. First, I want you to know you're not alone in feeling this way. Many students face challenges with certain subjects, including chemistry. But there's something important I'd like to talk to you about: self-efficacy.
- Shanika: Self-Efficacy? What's that?
- Ms. Kohl: Self-Efficacy is the belief in your abilities to achieve goals and overcome challenges. It's about having confidence in yourself and your capability to succeed. Developing self-efficacy can make a big difference in how you approach your studies. Instead of feeling overwhelmed, you can believe in your capacity to learn and improve.
- Shanika: That sounds great, Ms. Kohl. But how can I employ self-efficacy in school?
- Ms. Kohl: Excellent question, Shanika. Here are a few specific ways you can employ self-efficacy in your school life:

- Set Realistic Goals: Break down your learning objectives into smaller, achievable steps. Start with manageable goals; as you accomplish them, you'll build confidence and motivation to tackle more challenging tasks.
- Embrace a Growth Mindset: Understand that your intelligence and abilities can grow through effort and practice. Don't view setbacks as failures but rather as opportunities for growth. With this mindset, you can overcome obstacles and learn from your mistakes.
- Seek Support: Don't hesitate to reach out for help when you need it. Speak with your teachers, like Mr. Miller, about your struggles in chemistry. They may provide additional explanations or resources to aid your understanding.
- Build a Study Routine: Establish a consistent study routine that includes dedicated time for reviewing and practicing chemistry concepts. Sticking to a schedule will reinforce your belief in your abilities, and you'll see progress over time.
- Celebrate Small Victories: Recognize and celebrate your achievements along the way. Acknowledge the effort you put into your studies and reward yourself when you reach milestones. This positive reinforcement will enhance your self-belief.

- Shanika: Thank you, Ms. Kohl. I never realized how important self-efficacy could be. I'll try these strategies and believe in my ability to succeed in chemistry.
- Ms. Kohl: You're welcome, Shanika. Remember that developing self-efficacy is a journey, and it takes time. Believe in yourself, stay motivated, and keep pushing forward. I have confidence that you can overcome this challenge. And if you ever need someone to talk to or further guidance, don't hesitate to come back and see me.
- Shanika: Thank you so much, Ms. Kohl. I appreciate your support and advice. I'll build my self-efficacy and tackle chemistry with a positive mindset.
- Ms. Kohl: That's the spirit, Shanika! I'm here to support you every step of the way. You've got this!

Group Discussion:

After the role-play activity, take some time to reflect as a group on the discussion and consider how you can apply the concepts discussed in your educational context. Think about the crucial role of teacher behaviors in promoting student wellness, including connectedness, self-efficacy, and socio-emotional well-being. Brainstorm together and explore strategies and interventions that can be implemented to improve the socio-emotional well-being of your students, such as mentorship programs, creating positive classroom environments, and fostering strong teacher-student relationships. By taking action based on these reflections, you can work toward creating a supportive and Transformative Educational experience for your students.

Role-Play 2

Title: Guiding Students toward Connectedness

Objective: The five-minute role-play exercise demonstrates how a caring school principal encourages a student to join a school club. He hopes to help the student feel connected and accepted by doing so.

Roles:
- Jamal: eighth-grade student
- Principal Sommers: school principal

Instructions:

Setting the Scene:
- Jamal makes an appointment to see Principal Sommers. Jamal knocks on the door and enters Principal Sommers's office.

Role-Playing Process:
- Principal Sommers: (Smiling) Welcome, Jamal. Please have a seat. I heard you wanted to discuss some struggles you've been facing with making friends and finding a real connection here at school. I'm here to listen and offer support. Would you be willing to tell me a little more about what you are struggling with lately?
- Jamal: Thank you, Principal Sommers. I've been feeling a bit overwhelmed lately. I've been having trouble connecting with others, affecting my school experience. I feel like I don't belong, and it's hard to focus on my studies.
- Principal Sommers: I appreciate your honesty, Jamal. Feeling connected is an important part of student wellness. Can you tell me more about the challenges you've been facing regarding connectedness?
- Jamal: I've been having trouble making friends and building relationships with students and teachers. It feels like I'm on the outside looking in. I don't feel like I belong to the school community, and it's been affecting my motivation to participate in class and complete my homework.
- Principal Sommers: I understand how that can be tough, Jamal. Feeling connected is crucial for your well-being and academic success. Knowing you're not alone in experiencing these feelings

is essential. Many students face similar challenges. We can work together to address this. Have you ever considered joining any clubs or extracurricular activities?
- Jamal: I haven't thought about it. I'm unsure if I'd fit in or find something interesting.
- Principal Sommers: Exploring different activities can be a great way to meet new people with similar interests. Finding a club or group where you feel connected and accepted might surprise you. We have a variety of clubs here at the school, ranging from sports to robotics and arts. I can help you find one that aligns with your interests.
- Jamal: That sounds like a good idea. I've always been interested in robotics. Maybe I could give that a try.
- Principal Sommers: Excellent choice, Jamal! The robotics club is a welcoming community where students work together on exciting projects. I'm confident you'll find a sense of belonging there. Additionally, I encourage you to contact your teachers if you need academic or emotional support. They are here to help you succeed.
- Jamal: Thank you, Principal Sommers. I appreciate your guidance and support. I'll consider joining the robotics club and reaching out to my teachers.
- Principal Sommers: You're welcome, Jamal. Remember that we're here for you every step of the way. Building connections takes time, but with a little effort and openness, you can find your place within the school community. Stay positive, believe in yourself, and don't hesitate to seek support when you need it. Together, we'll work toward improving your socio-emotional well-being and academic achievement.
- Jamal: I will, Principal Sommers. Thank you again for taking the time to listen and guide me.
- Principal Sommers: It's my pleasure, Jamal. We're a team, and I'm here to support you. Please don't hesitate to reach out if you ever need to talk further or have any other concerns.

Group Discussion:

After the role-play activity, take some time to reflect as a group on the discussion and consider how you can apply the concepts discussed in your educational context. Think about the crucial role of teacher behaviors in promoting student wellness, including connectedness, self-efficacy, and socio-emotional well-being. Brainstorm together and explore strategies and interventions that can be implemented to improve the socio-emotional well-being of your students, such as mentorship programs, creating positive classroom environments, and fostering strong teacher-student relationships. By taking action based on these reflections, you can work toward creating a supportive and transformative educational experience for your students.

Role-Play 3

Title: Teacher and Department Chair Discussing Socio-Emotional Well-Being

Objective: The five-minute role-play shows collaboration between a teacher and her department chair to ensure socio-emotional well-being for students.

Roles:
- Miss Sanders: teacher
- Mrs. Smank: World Language department chair

Instructions:

Setting the Scene: Miss Sanders knocks on Mrs. Smank's office door and enters.

Role-Playing Process:
- Miss Sanders: Good morning, Mrs. Smank. Thank you for taking the time to meet with me today. I wanted to discuss some concerns I have about the socio-emotional well-being of my eleventh-grade students.
- Mrs. Smank: Of course, Miss Sanders. I'm glad you brought this up. What specifically are you observing in your students that has raised these concerns?
- Miss Sanders: Well, I've noticed that some students lack a sense of connectedness to the school community. They don't seem to feel like they belong, and their relationships with staff and peers appear strained. This is affecting their motivation to learn and even their reading achievement.
- Mrs. Smank: That's a valid concern, Miss Sanders. Connectedness plays a vital role in student well-being and academic success. I'm glad you're addressing this. What strategies have you tried to foster a sense of connectedness among your students?
- Miss Sanders: I've been trying to build strong relationships with my students, both inside and outside the classroom. I've also encouraged them to participate in extracurricular activities and connect with other students who share their interests. However, we could do more as a school to promote a sense of belonging and support.

- Mrs. Smank: I agree, Miss Sanders. Educators must create an environment where students feel valued, supported, and connected. Have you come across any research or strategies that could help us improve the socio-emotional well-being of our students?
- Miss Sanders: Yes, I have. One approach that has shown promising results is adult mentoring. Studies have found that students who receive personalized academic assistance and socio-emotional support from teachers, counselors, and other staff members experience decreased levels of depression and an increased sense of belonging. Perhaps we could implement a mentorship program to support our students.
- Mrs. Smank: That's an excellent idea, Miss Sanders. A mentorship program could help foster stronger relationships between students and staff members, providing the support and guidance they need. We could also explore other interventions to build socio-emotional skills, such as cooperative learning and creating positive classroom environments.
- Miss Sanders: Absolutely. I think implementing these strategies would improve our students' socio-emotional well-being and positively impact their academic performance. When students feel connected and supported, they are more likely to be engaged in the classroom and persist in learning.
- Mrs. Smank: I couldn't agree more, Miss Sanders. Let's work together to develop a comprehensive plan to address these concerns. We can start by researching successful mentorship programs and interventions that have been proven effective in promoting socio-emotional skills. Additionally, we should involve other teachers and staff members to ensure a collaborative effort.
- Miss Sanders: That sounds like a solid plan, Mrs. Smank. By prioritizing the socio-emotional well-being of our students, we can create a nurturing environment where they can thrive academically and personally.
- Mrs. Smank: I'm glad you're passionate about this, Miss Sanders. I believe that by focusing on transformational teacher behaviors and implementing strategies to improve student wellness, we can make

a real difference in the lives of our students. Let's continue this conversation and develop a comprehensive action plan.
- Miss Sanders: Thank you, Mrs. Smank. I'm excited to collaborate with you on this critical initiative. Together, we can create a positive and supportive learning environment that truly transforms the educational experience for our students.

They continue their discussion, brainstorming ideas and strategies to improve the socio-emotional well-being of their students.

Group Discussion:
After the role-play activity, take some time to reflect as a group on the discussion and consider how you can apply the concepts discussed in your educational context. Think about the crucial role of teacher behaviors in promoting student wellness, including connectedness, self-efficacy, and socio-emotional well-being. Brainstorm together and explore strategies and interventions that can be implemented to improve the socio-emotional well-being of your students, such as mentorship programs, creating positive classroom environments, and fostering strong teacher-student relationships. By acting based on these reflections, you can work toward creating a supportive and transformative educational experience for your students.

Section 3H:
Interdisciplinary and Collaborative Lesson Planning

The following may be used by school departments, by faculty, or for school-wide initiatives. These activities guide teachers in designing lesson plans using the theories and strategies discussed in the textbook. They may involve creating objectives, selecting appropriate instructional methods, developing assessment strategies, and adapting content for diverse learners.

Lesson Plan 1

Title: Exploring *The Sun Does Shine*: Interdisciplinary Lesson Plan

Grade Level: 9th–12th Grade

Content Areas: History, Science, English Language Arts (ELA)

Lesson Objectives:
- Students will analyze the themes and content of *The Sun Does Shine* and make connections to historical events, scientific concepts, and literary techniques.
- Students will explore the impact of systemic injustice on individuals and society, promoting empathy and critical thinking.
- Students will apply principles of interdisciplinary learning to develop a deeper understanding of the book's themes and engage in cross-curricular connections.

Instructional Methods:
- Prereading Activity: Introduce the book's historical context, focusing on the Civil Rights Movement and the criminal justice system. Engage students in a whole-class discussion about the importance of justice and its impact on society.
- Literature Analysis: Assign reading of *The Sun Does Shine*, with students analyzing literary techniques, themes, and character development. Incorporate guided discussions and journaling to deepen their comprehension and critical thinking skills.
- History Connection: Engage students in researching and presenting on historical events related to systemic racism, wrongful convictions, or social justice movements. Facilitate discussions on the parallels between the book and real-world events.
- Science Connection: Explore scientific concepts presented in the book, such as forensic science, DNA analysis, or psychology. Conduct experiments or simulations related to these concepts to deepen students' understanding and engagement.
- Group Projects: Divide students into interdisciplinary groups and assign each group a theme from the book (e.g., resilience, hope, forgiveness). Students will create presentations or artistic

representations incorporating elements from history, science, and literary analysis to explore the theme's significance.

Assessment Strategies:
- Formative Assessment: Monitor students' engagement, participation, and critical thinking during discussions, activities, and group work.
- Literary Analysis Essay: Have students write an essay analyzing the book's themes, literary techniques, and connections to historical events and scientific concepts.
- Group Presentation: Evaluate each group's presentation on their assigned theme, assessing their ability to incorporate interdisciplinary elements and effectively communicate their findings.
- Reflection and Empathy: Assign students a reflective writing task where they discuss their emotional responses to the book and their understanding of the impacts of systemic injustice. Assess their ability to empathize and think critically.
- Self-Assessment: Provide students with rubrics or self-assessment tools to evaluate their interdisciplinary learning skills, collaboration, and growth throughout the unit.

Adapting Content for Diverse Learners:
- Visual Learners: Utilize visual aids, graphic organizers, and multimedia resources to support understanding and engagement in the book's themes and interdisciplinary connections.
- Auditory Learners: Incorporate audio recordings, interviews, or dramatic readings related to the book and historical events to enhance listening skills and promote comprehension.
- Kinesthetic Learners: Incorporate hands-on activities, role-plays, or simulations that allow students to engage with the content and themes of the book physically.
- English Language Learners: Provide bilingual resources, simplified language versions of the book, and opportunities for peer collaboration to support comprehension and language acquisition.
- Students with Special Needs: Offer additional support, accommodations, and modified assignments based on individual learning needs to ensure access to the book and promote engagement in interdisciplinary activities.

Using *The Sun Does Shine* as a catalyst, this interdisciplinary lesson plan aims to promote deep learning, critical thinking, and empathy across history, science, and ELA. Students will analyze literature, explore historical contexts, and connect scientific concepts while applying principles of interdisciplinary learning. The plan accommodates diverse learners, fostering a comprehensive understanding of systemic injustice and its impact on individuals and society.

Lesson Plan 2

Title: Exploring Intersectionality and Feminist Perspectives: Lessons Inspired by A *Feminist Manifesto in Fifteen Suggestions*

Grade Level: Department-wide/Faculty-wide/School-wide

Subject Areas: Sociology, Women's Studies, African American History

Lesson Objectives:
- Students will understand the principles of feminism and intersectionality.
- Students will analyze the relevance of feminist perspectives in sociology, women's studies, and African American history.
- Students will apply the theories and strategies discussed in A *Feminist Manifesto in Fifteen Suggestions* to their respective disciplines.

Instructional Methods:
- Whole-Group Discussion: Engage students in discussing feminism, intersectionality, and the key ideas presented in A *Feminist Manifesto in Fifteen Suggestions*.
- Literature Circles: Divide students into small groups, assigning each group a chapter or suggestion from the manifesto to read and discuss. Students can identify connections to their respective subjects and present their findings to the larger group.
- Interactive Lectures: Conduct presentations or panel discussions where experts in sociology, women's studies, and African American history discuss the relevance of feminist perspectives and intersectionality in their fields.
- Research Projects: Assign students individual or group research projects where they explore the impact of feminist movements and intersectional analysis in specific historical events, social issues, or cultural contexts related to sociology, women's studies, or African American history.
- Creative Projects: Encourage students to express their understanding of feminism and intersectionality through creative mediums such as artwork, poetry, short films, or dramatic performances.

Assessment Strategies:
- Formative Assessment: Observe students' engagement, participation, and critical thinking skills during whole-group discussions, literature circles, and interactive lectures.
- Group Presentation: Evaluate each group's presentation on their assigned chapter or suggestion from the manifesto, assessing their understanding of the concepts and ability to connect to their respective subjects.
- Research Project Assessment: Assess individual or group research projects based on their research skills, ability to analyze and synthesize information, and incorporation of feminist perspectives and intersectional analysis.
- Creative Project Assessment: Evaluate creative projects based on students' ability to express feminist perspectives and intersectionality through their chosen medium, demonstrating their understanding of the subject matter.
- Reflective Writing: Assign students a reflective essay or journal entry where they discuss the impact of feminist perspectives and intersectionality on their understanding of their respective subjects.

Adapting Content for Diverse Learners:
- Visual Learners: Provide visual aids, infographics, or multimedia resources to enhance understanding of feminist theories, intersectionality, and their applications across disciplines.
- Auditory Learners: Include audio recordings, guest speakers, or opportunities for class discussions and debates to engage students' listening skills and foster dialogue around feminist perspectives and intersectionality.
- Kinesthetic Learners: Incorporate interactive activities, role-plays, or simulations that allow students to physically engage with the concepts of feminism, intersectionality, and their applications in various disciplines.
- English Language Learners: Offer bilingual resources, simplified language versions of texts, and opportunities for peer collaboration to support comprehension and language acquisition.

- Students with Special Needs: Provide additional support, such as graphic organizers, guided prompts, or modified assignments, based on individual learning needs and accommodations.

By exploring the principles of feminism, intersectionality, and A *Feminist Manifesto in Fifteen Suggestions* across disciplines, this lesson plan aims to foster a school-wide understanding of feminist perspectives and their applications. Students will engage in critical thinking, research, creative expression, and diverse learning styles, promoting a deeper understanding of the impact of feminism and intersectionality in sociology, women's studies, and African American history.

Lesson Plan 3

Title: Exploring Plato's Allegory of the Cave: A Cross-Disciplinary Lesson Plan

Grade Level: 9th–12th Grade

Subject Areas: History, Theology, English Language Arts (ELA)

Lesson Objectives:
- Students will analyze Plato's Allegory of the Cave and its relevance to various disciplines.
- Students will apply critical thinking skills to interpret the allegory and draw connections to historical events, theological concepts, and literary elements.
- Students will engage in cross-disciplinary discussions and collaborative activities to deepen their understanding of the allegory's themes and implications.

Instructional Methods:
- Whole-Group Reading: Introduce Plato's Allegory of the Cave to students, providing context and discussing its significance in philosophy, history, theology, and literature.
- Cross-Disciplinary Group Discussions: Divide students into small groups, assigning each group a specific discipline (history, theology, ELA). Encourage students to discuss and analyze the allegory through the lens of their assigned discipline, considering historical events, theological concepts, and literary elements.
- Jigsaw Activity: Reorganize the groups to create mixed-discipline groups. Have students share their insights and perspectives with members from different disciplines, facilitating cross-disciplinary discussions and collaborative learning.
- Analysis and Reflection: Assign individual or group tasks where students analyze specific aspects of the allegory related to their discipline. For example, history students may examine historical parallels, theology students may explore theological implications, and ELA students may analyze literary devices used by Plato.
- Culminating Project: In cross-disciplinary groups, have students design and present a project that showcases their collective

understanding of the allegory's relevance across disciplines. This may include presentations, creative interpretations, or multimedia projects.

Assessment Strategies:
- Cross-Disciplinary Discussions: Assess students' participation and engagement in cross-disciplinary discussions, evaluating their ability to draw connections between the allegory and different disciplines.
- Individual or Group Analysis: Evaluate students' written or oral analyses of specific aspects of the allegory, focusing on their ability to apply critical thinking skills and disciplinary knowledge.
- Culminating Project: Assess students' final projects based on their depth of understanding, creativity, and ability to communicate the allegory's relevance to multiple disciplines effectively.

Adapting Content for Diverse Learners:
- Visual Learners: Utilize visual aids, such as diagrams or infographics, to illustrate the allegory's concepts and support understanding across disciplines.
- Auditory Learners: Provide audio recordings or engage in class discussions, encouraging students to express their interpretations and engage in cross-disciplinary conversations.
- Kinesthetic Learners: Incorporate hands-on activities, such as role-plays or creative projects, that allow students to embody the allegory's themes and concepts physically.
- English Language Learners: Offer bilingual resources, simplified language versions of texts, and opportunities for peer collaboration to support comprehension and language acquisition across disciplines.
- Students with Special Needs: Provide additional support, such as graphic organizers, modified assignments, or personalized accommodations, based on individual learning needs to ensure access to the allegory and its relevance to multiple disciplines.

This lesson plan aims to foster a deeper understanding of the allegory's themes and implications across different academic disciplines by exploring Plato's Allegory of the Cave through cross-disciplinary lenses of history, theology, and ELA. Students will engage in critical thinking, collaborative learning, and diverse learning styles, encouraging a holistic approach to their education and applying interdisciplinary knowledge.

Sample Template across three disciplines: Business, ELA, and Mathematics

Title: Applying Student Wellness Principles: Lessons from [Book Title] in Business, Math, and ELA

Grade Level: [Appropriate grade levels]

Subject Areas: Business, Math, ELA

Lesson Objectives:
- Students will explore key concepts and themes from [Book Title] and apply them to business, math, and ELA disciplines.
- Students will analyze the relevance of student wellness principles in the context of the book's content.
- Students will apply principles of student wellness to enhance learning, critical thinking, and personal development across multiple disciplines.

Instructional Methods:
- Whole-Group Discussion: Engage students in a discussion about the central ideas, themes, and messages conveyed in [Book Title] and the relevance of these concepts to business, math, and ELA.

Interdisciplinary Activities:
- Business: Assign students a project to create a business plan inspired by a concept or scenario from the book, incorporating financial literacy and entrepreneurial skills.
- Math: Provide students with real-world math problems related to topics in the book, such as calculating statistics, creating budgets, or analyzing data.
- ELA: Have students analyze excerpts from the book, focusing on literary devices, character development, or themes, and create written responses or presentations.
- Collaborative Projects: Organize cross-disciplinary groups where students work together to apply concepts from the book to solve complex problems or create multimedia presentations.

- Reflection and Self-Assessment: Integrate opportunities for students to reflect on their learning experiences, evaluate their well-being, and set personal goals for growth and academic achievement.
- Differentiated Instruction: Adapt instructional strategies, materials, and assessments to accommodate diverse learners across the disciplines of business, math, and ELA.

Assessment Strategies:
- Formative Assessment: Observe students' active participation, engagement, and application of student wellness principles during discussions, collaborative projects, and interdisciplinary activities.
- Performance Tasks: Assess students' ability to apply concepts from [Book Title] to their respective disciplines through projects, presentations, or written assignments.
- Self-Assessment: Provide self-assessment tools or reflection prompts for students to evaluate their well-being, their progress, and the effectiveness of applying student wellness principles in their learning process.
- Peer Assessment: Encourage students to provide constructive feedback and support their peers in applying student wellness principles across different disciplines.
- Summative Assessment: Evaluate students' overall understanding of the book's content and ability to apply student wellness principles to business, math, and ELA through exams, essays, or presentations.

Adapting Content for Diverse Learners:
- Visual Learners: Incorporate visual aids, diagrams, charts, or infographics to enhance understanding of concepts and facilitate connections between the book's content and business, math, and ELA disciplines.
- Auditory Learners: Include audio recordings, oral presentations, or discussions to engage students' listening skills and promote comprehension of the book's content across multiple disciplines.
- Kinesthetic Learners: Design hands-on activities, simulations, or role-plays that allow students to physically engage with the book's content and apply student wellness principles in business, math, and ELA.

- English Language Learners: Provide bilingual resources, simplified language versions of texts, and opportunities for peer collaboration to support comprehension, language acquisition, and interdisciplinary connections.
- Students with Special Needs: Offer additional support, accommodations, and modified assignments based on individual learning needs to ensure access to the book's content and student wellness principles across diverse disciplines.

By integrating the principles of student wellness and the content of [Book Title] across business, math, and ELA disciplines, this lesson plan aims to foster interdisciplinary connections, critical thinking, and personal growth among students. It provides a framework for department-wide, faculty-wide, or school-wide implementation, promoting a holistic approach to education and empowering students to apply their learning across various disciplines.

Chapter 4
Improving Student Performance

This chapter contains several exercises and applications to help teachers apply the theoretical content found in chapter 4 of the accompanying foundational text, *An Introduction to Transformational Education*. These exercises are designed to enhance understanding, promote critical thinking, and provide practical examples for educators. These various applications and exercises in educational theory textbooks aim to bridge the gap between theory and practice, allowing teachers to actively engage with the content and apply it to their teaching contexts.

- **Section 4A: Self-Assessment and Reflection**
- **Section 4B: Case Studies**
- **Section 4C: Lesson Planning Activities**
- **Section 4D: Reflection and Discussion**
- **Section 4E: Peer Mentorship**
- **Section 4F: Scenarios**
- **Section 4G: Role-Playing**
- **Section 4H: Interdisciplinary and Collaborative Lesson Planning**

Section 4A:
Self-Assessment and Reflection

The Student Performance Self-Assessment is a tool that allows educators to evaluate the promotion of student performance in their school context. This activity provides self-assessment prompts to help teachers reflect on their instructional practices, beliefs, and professional growth. It will encourage educators to evaluate their strengths, identify improvement areas, and set further development goals. **This self-assessment consists of three sections: Engagement, Academic Performance, and Prosocial Behaviors.** Each section contains a series of statements related to the respective category.

Student Performance Self-Assessment

Instructions: For each statement, indicate your level of agreement or frequency of practice.

5—Strongly Agree, 4—Agree, 3—Neutral, 2—Disagree, 1—Strongly Disagree

Engagement

Engagement is the highly valued outcome, which refers to the degree to which a student is involved and immersed in the work of meaningful learning. Engagement includes activities that promote progress in education, such as feeling motivated to complete homework or paying attention to classroom activities in an observable way. It might also be being able to self-monitor comprehension or articulate one's progress in learning. Engagement may also be measured by a student's apparent compliance with directions and a discernible intent to learn.

_____ 1. I actively promote meaningful learning experiences in the classroom.

_____ 2. I encourage and motivate students to complete their homework and assignments.

_____ 3. I observe and recognize students' attention and participation in classroom activities.

_____ 4. I help students develop self-monitoring skills to assess their comprehension progress.

_____ 5. I encourage students to articulate their progress and learning experiences.

_____ 6. I provide clear and effective directions for classroom activities.

_____ 7. I observe apparent compliance with directions and a genuine intent to learn from students.

_____ 8. I aim to create a positive and engaging classroom environment.

_____ 9. I recognize the impact of transformational school leadership on student engagement.

_____ 10. I believe that increasing student engagement leads to improved student performance outcomes.

Engagement Total Score _____/50

Academic Performance

Within Transformational Education, academic performance refers to demonstrated skill and proficiency in written work, academic quality, and durability of learning. We understand this to mean knowledge retained and abilities gained, maintained, and used over time.

_____ 1. I consistently provide clear and constructive feedback on students' written work and assignments.

_____ 2. I create a learning environment that fosters academic quality and encourages students to excel.

_____ 3. I regularly assess and monitor students' progress to ensure that they are on track with their learning goals.

_____ 4. I provide personalized support and assistance to students who may be struggling academically.

_____ 5. I encourage a growth mindset, emphasizing the importance of effort and resilience in the learning process.

_____ 6. I foster a learning climate that promotes curiosity and a love for learning among students.

_____ 7. I actively engage students in meaningful discussions and activities to enhance their understanding of the subject.

_____ 8. I create opportunities for students to apply their knowledge and skills in real-world contexts.

_____ 9. I am approachable and available to support students outside regular class hours when they need extra help.

_____ 10. I continuously seek professional development to enhance my teaching strategies and academic support techniques.

Academic Performance Total Score _____/50

Prosocial Behaviors

Prosocial behavior can be generalized as concern for others. It means caring about other people's feelings, well-being, and rights. Actions intended to help people are prosocial; examples include helping, comforting, working together, collaborating, and sharing.

_____ 1. I prioritize fostering empathy and kindness as essential outcomes in my classroom.

_____ 2. I actively model empathetic behavior and emotional communication with my students.

_____ 3. I encourage and facilitate opportunities for students to collaborate and work together.

_____ 4. I recognize and acknowledge acts of kindness and prosocial behavior in my students.

_____ 5. I promote an inclusive classroom environment where students, even those from different groups, accept and support one another.

_____ 6. I integrate discussions or activities that help students understand and respect each other's feelings and rights.

_____ 7. I provide personalized support and guidance to students needing help with prosocial behaviors.

_____ 8. I encourage my students to show kindness and consideration for others daily.

_____ 9. I facilitate opportunities for students to engage in prosocial actions, such as helping those in need or consoling someone upset.

_____ 10. I believe that fostering prosocial behaviors is crucial for student success in education and life.

Prosocial Behaviors Total Score _____/50

Interpretation of Scores by Section:

Scoring:
- Add up your scores for all the statements.
- The higher the total score, the more you practice the target teacher behavior in the classroom.

Interpretation:
- 41–50: You effectively incorporate the target teacher behavior strategies in your classroom.
- 31–40: Your use of the target teacher behavior in the classroom is moderate. Continue to build on your current strategies to enhance this behavior.
- 21–30: You have some level of the target teacher behavior in your classroom, but there is room for improvement.
- 10–20: Your use of the target teacher behavior in the classroom may be limited.

Note: This self-assessment tool is designed to provide a general indication of your current use of the Transformational Education target for the classroom or school context. It is not a comprehensive evaluation and should be used as a starting point for reflection and professional growth.

Individual Reflection Questions
Transformational Education and Student Performance

These questions encourage teachers to reflect on their teaching practices, beliefs, and experiences. They help educators connect theory to their instructional context and promote self-reflection and professional growth.

Instructions: Utilize the following questions to reflect on your current practices regarding student performance discussed in chapter 4 of *An Introduction to Transformational Education*. You are encouraged to write your thoughts down for later reflection and discussion with a mentor.

1. How do you currently measure student performance in your classroom or school? Are there any additional measures beyond traditional academic assessments that should be considered?

2. Reflect on the concept of engagement as a measure of student performance. How do you foster meaningful learning experiences that encourage student involvement and immersion in the subject matter?

3. In what ways do you see a connection between transformational school leadership and student engagement? How can transformational teacher leadership contribute to increased student engagement in your classroom?

4. How do you define academic performance in your educational setting? How can you ensure that students not only demonstrate knowledge but also retain and apply that knowledge over time?

5. Consider the role of teacher behaviors, such as authentic engagement, meaning making, personalized support, and stimulating curiosity, in influencing academic success among students. How can you incorporate these behaviors into your teaching approach?

6. Prosocial behaviors, such as empathy and kindness, are valued outcomes in the Transformational Education model. How can you actively cultivate empathy and kindness among your students? What strategies can you implement to encourage these behaviors in the classroom?

7. Are there any specific challenges you face in promoting prosocial behaviors in your classroom or school? How can you overcome these challenges and foster a culture of empathy and kindness?

8. In what ways do you believe social and emotional learning should be integrated into the curriculum to support holistic student development?

9. As an educator, how can you incorporate the principles of the Transformational Education model into your teaching practices to enhance student performance in academic, social, and emotional domains?

10. How do you observe students responding to one another in your classroom? Are there instances of empathy, kindness, and collaboration that you can foster and encourage further?

Section 4B:
Case Studies

Case studies present real or hypothetical scenarios teachers may encounter in their classrooms. They require educators to analyze the situation, identify challenges, and propose solutions based on the theories and concepts discussed in the textbook.

Instructions: Read the provided case studies carefully. Take note of the critical points and details presented in the text. Aim to arrive at well-rounded and thoughtful answers that consider various perspectives. Refer to the case study as needed to support your responses.

To benefit from the case study of Mr. Christian and understand his employment or failure to employ crucial teacher behaviors, analyze Mr. Christian's practices of engagement, academic performance, and prosocial behaviors.

Mr. Christian

Mr. Christian, the tenth-grade geometry teacher, was unlike any other educator at Harmony High School. When he stepped into the classroom, his passion for teaching shone brightly in how he animatedly explained geometric concepts using visual aids and interactive demonstrations. He knew engaging students was key to their success, and he effortlessly captured their attention with his dynamic teaching style.

During class discussions, Mr. Christian didn't simply stand at the front and deliver lectures. Instead, he moved around the room, making eye contact with each student and encouraging them to share their thoughts and ideas. He listened intently, nodding in affirmation and praising their contributions, no matter how small. His genuine interest in their input made the students feel valued and motivated to participate actively.

One day, he noticed Muhammad, a quiet and reserved student, struggling with a complex proof. Instead of rushing to solve it for him, Mr. Christian quietly approached Muhammad's desk. Leaning in, he asked, "What's giving you trouble, Muhammad?" With patience and empathy, he guided Muhammad through each step, empowering him to solve the problem himself. As Muhammad's face lit up with understanding, Mr. Christian patted him on the back, acknowledging his effort.

Outside the classroom, Mr. Christian's dedication to nurturing his students' personal growth was equally evident. He organized weekly group activities that focused on building teamwork and collaboration. Through hands-on projects and games, he encouraged the students to work together, fostering a sense of camaraderie and trust among them.

One memorable afternoon, Mr. Christian took his students on a community service outing to a local shelter. Rather than merely telling them to be kind and empathetic, he led by example. He actively engaged with the shelter's residents, asking about their lives and listening to their stories. Inspired by their teacher's behavior, the students followed suit, showing genuine compassion and understanding to those they encountered.

As the school year progressed, the transformation in Mr. Christian's students was remarkable. Their academic performance improved significantly, but more importantly, they became more confident, empathetic, and prosocial. The classroom buzzed with positive energy as they supported each other, exchanged ideas, and celebrated their successes.

Other teachers and school staff couldn't help but notice the positive change in Mr. Christian's students. They observed how his engaging teaching style and compassionate interactions with students influenced their behavior in and out of the classroom. The students seemed to radiate a sense of community and kindness, creating a school atmosphere that was vibrant and inclusive.

As the year drew to a close, Mr. Christian knew that his impact reached far beyond the subject of geometry. He had instilled a love for learning, empathy, and prosocial behavior in his students. With a heart full of pride, he waved goodbye to them on the last day of school, knowing that they were not just well prepared academically but also equipped with the essential qualities to lead healthy and fulfilling lives.

Discuss:

In reflecting on Mr. Christian's teaching practices, share examples of how he effectively promotes engagement, academic performance, and prosocial behaviors in his classroom. Additionally, identify instances where Mr. Christian falls short in addressing these elements and suggest alternative strategies he could employ to improve student performance.

Ms. Santos

Ms. Santos, a new seventh-grade science teacher, entered her classroom with a warm smile and a genuine desire to make a positive impact. She aimed to foster engagement and meaningful learning experiences among her students, but as the weeks passed, her efforts seemed to fall flat.

In class, Ms. Santos tried various strategies and activities, hoping to motivate her students to participate actively. However, their responses were lackluster, and their body language conveyed boredom and disinterest. Even during hands-on experiments, some students merely went through the motions, their eyes wandering away from the tasks.

As the days passed, Ms. Santos observed her students struggling to self-monitor their comprehension. When she asked them about their progress in learning, their responses were vague and hesitant. It was clear they lacked the metacognitive skills needed to articulate their understanding and progress effectively.

Ms. Santos attempted to communicate clearly with her students, but her directions often confused them. As she explained complex concepts, she noticed some students staring blankly, struggling to follow her explanations. The lack of engagement was evident, and many students seemed disconnected from the lessons.

She tried to inspire and motivate her students through Transformational Leadership behaviors, but her words failed to resonate. Instead of enthusiastic faces, she saw blank expressions and restless movements. The energy in the classroom remained low, and her attempts to create excitement were met with indifference.

Though she introduced what she believed were innovative teaching methods, the students' responses were far from enthusiastic. The once-vibrant experiments now felt mundane, and the classroom atmosphere lacked the curiosity and eagerness she had hoped to instill.

Despite her intentions to support and acknowledge her students' efforts, Ms. Santos struggled to connect with them on a deeper level. Her praise felt superficial, and the lack of genuine recognition left her students feeling unappreciated and unmotivated.

In her pursuit of promoting prosocial behavior, Ms. Santos organized group projects and discussions on helping others. However, collaboration seemed forced, and some students preferred to work alone rather than engage with their peers. The atmosphere lacked the sense of community she had hoped to foster.

As the school assessed academic performance through various methods, it became evident that Ms. Santos's students were not progressing significantly. Their grades remained stagnant, and standardized test scores showed minimal improvement. It was clear that her teaching approach was not effectively helping them grasp the subject matter.

Despite her good intentions, Ms. Santos's inability to effectively promote student performance, engagement, and prosocial behavior left her feeling disheartened. The classroom she had envisioned as a vibrant hub of enthusiastic learners had become a place of indifference and stagnation. She knew she needed to reassess her methods and find ways to connect with her students and genuinely inspire them to learn. Only then could she make the positive impact she had hoped for.

Discuss:

In reflecting on Ms. Santos's teaching practices, share examples of how she effectively promoted or failed to promote engagement, academic performance, and prosocial behaviors in her classroom.

Section 4C:
Lesson Planning Activities

These activities guide teachers in designing lesson plans using the theories and strategies discussed in the textbook. They may involve creating objectives, selecting appropriate instructional methods, developing assessment strategies, and adapting content for diverse learners.

Instructions: Use the following examples to guide you in your lesson planning.

Example 1

Grade Level: 7th Grade

Subject: Science

Lesson Title: Exploring the Deserts of the World with Empathy and Kindness

Duration: 60 minutes

Objective:
- Students will demonstrate an understanding of the geographical locations and characteristics of various deserts worldwide.
- Students will apply the principles of empathy and kindness in their interactions with their peers during group activities.
- Students will demonstrate engagement and active participation in the lesson.

Instructional Methods:
- Brainstorming: Begin the lesson by asking students what they know about deserts and list their responses on the board.
- Multimedia Presentation: Use interactive visuals and videos to introduce different deserts and their unique features.
- Group Discussions: Organize students into small groups to discuss the challenges and adaptations of plants, animals, and people in desert environments.
- Empathy Role-Play: Engage students in role-playing scenarios to understand the challenges desert communities face and encourage empathetic responses.
- Mapping Activity: Provide students with world maps and have them locate and label major deserts around the globe.
- Virtual Desert Tour: Utilize virtual reality (VR) technology or online resources to give students a virtual tour of a desert, enhancing their understanding and engagement.
- Hands-On Desert Experiment: Conduct a simple desert-themed experiment, like building a miniature desert ecosystem, to deepen their knowledge.

Assessment Strategies:
- Group Presentations: Have each group present their findings about a specific desert, including its location, climate, and unique features.
- Empathy Reflection: After the role-playing activity, facilitate a discussion to reflect on how empathy can make a positive impact on the lives of people living in harsh environments like deserts.
- Mapping Quiz: Administer a quiz to assess students' ability to locate and label major deserts on a world map accurately.
- Desert Ecosystem Report: Ask students to create a report on the desert ecosystem they built during the hands-on experiment, explaining the components and interactions within it.

Adapting Content for Diverse Learners:
- Visual Learners: Provide plenty of multimedia resources, such as videos and images, to enhance understanding for visual learners.
- Auditory Learners: Use clear verbal explanations and encourage class discussions to engage auditory learners effectively.
- Kinesthetic Learners: Incorporate hands-on activities, like the desert ecosystem experiment, to cater to kinesthetic learners' needs.
- English Language Learners (ELL): Offer simplified language and provide vocabulary support to accommodate ELL students in understanding the lesson content.

Integration of Prosocial Behaviors:
- Classroom Norms: Establish a positive and inclusive classroom environment by discussing the importance of empathy, kindness, and respect for one another.
- Cooperative Learning: Promote teamwork and collaboration during group activities, encouraging students to listen to and support each other's ideas.
- Empathy Practice: Integrate empathy-building activities into the lesson, such as discussing people's challenges in deserts and brainstorming solutions.
- Kindness Journal: Encourage students to keep a kindness journal where they record acts of kindness they have witnessed or performed throughout the week.

Note: By integrating the principles of empathy and kindness into the lesson, students not only gain knowledge about the deserts of the world but also develop a deeper understanding of the challenges faced by different communities. The focus on prosocial behaviors and engagement helps create a positive learning environment, promoting holistic growth and character development among students.

Example 2

Grade Level: 10th Grade

Subject: Biology

Lesson Title: Exploring Animal Classification with Collaborative Learning

Duration: 60 minutes

Objective:
- Students will understand the principles of animal classification and be able to identify major animal groups based on their characteristics.
- Students will collaborate in small groups to research and create presentations on specific animal groups, fostering teamwork and communication skills.
- Students will apply critical thinking skills to analyze and compare the features of different animal groups.

Instructional Methods:
- Preassessment: Begin the lesson by conducting a short quiz to gauge students' prior knowledge of animal classification.
- Interactive Lecture: Present an engaging lecture on the principles of animal classification, including the main criteria for grouping animals into different categories.
- Group Research Activity: Divide students into small groups and assign each group a specific animal group (e.g., mammals, birds, reptiles, amphibians, fish, or invertebrates). Provide them with textbooks, online resources, and scientific articles to research and gather information about their assigned group.
- Collaborative Presentations: Instruct each group to create a presentation highlighting the defining characteristics, examples, and unique features of their assigned animal group. Encourage the use of multimedia elements to enhance their presentations.
- Gallery Walk: After the presentations are ready, set up a gallery walk where each group displays their work, and students can rotate to learn about other animal groups.
- Comparative Analysis: Lead a class discussion on the similarities and differences among the various animal groups, emphasizing

the adaptive features that help them survive in their respective environments.
- Classification Game: Organize a fun and interactive game where students classify pictures of animals into the appropriate groups based on their characteristics.

Assessment Strategies:
- Group Presentations: Assess each group's presentation based on accuracy, depth of research, and effective communication.
- Comparative Analysis Worksheet: Provide a worksheet with questions about the similarities and differences between animal groups for students to complete during the class discussion.
- Classification Game: Observe students' participation and accuracy during the classification game to assess their understanding of the content.
- Summative Assessment: Administer a written test to evaluate students' knowledge of animal classification, including identifying specific characteristics of different animal groups.

Adapting Content for Diverse Learners:
- Visual Learners: Incorporate visuals, diagrams, and charts in the lecture and presentations to aid visual learners in understanding the content.
- Auditory Learners: Ensure clear and concise verbal explanations during the lecture and discussions for auditory learners to grasp the concepts effectively.
- Kinesthetic Learners: Include hands-on activities, such as the classification game, to engage kinesthetic learners and reinforce their learning.
- English Language Learners (ELL): Provide vocabulary support and use simplified language when explaining complex biological terms.

Integration of Prosocial Behaviors:
- Group Dynamics: Emphasize the importance of teamwork and cooperation during the group research and presentation.

- Active Listening: Encourage students to actively listen to their peers' presentations and ask thoughtful questions to promote respectful and supportive behavior.
- Inclusivity: Ensure that all group members are actively involved and have equal opportunities to contribute to the collaborative activities.

Note: By exploring animal classification through collaborative learning, students not only gain a comprehensive understanding of the diversity of the animal kingdom but also develop essential skills such as teamwork, critical thinking, and effective communication. Integrating prosocial behaviors fosters a positive and inclusive classroom climate, enhancing the overall learning experience for tenth-grade biology students.

Example 3

Grade Level: 12th Grade

Subject: English Language

Lesson Title: Celebrating Maya Angelou: Exploring Themes and Impact in Her Literary Works

Duration: 60 minutes

Objective:
- Students will gain a deep understanding of the life and literary contributions of Maya Angelou, focusing on key themes and the impact of her works on society.
- Students will critically analyze selected poems and excerpts from Angelou's autobiographies to identify recurring themes and literary techniques.
- Students will express their insights through class discussions and creative writing, reflecting on the significance of Angelou's works in contemporary society.

Instructional Methods:
- Biography and Context: Begin the lesson with a multimedia presentation or video on Maya Angelou's life, highlighting her background, her experiences, and the historical context that influenced her writing.
- Close Reading of Selected Works: Provide students with excerpts from Angelou's autobiographies (*I Know Why the Caged Bird Sings, Gather Together in My Name,* or others) and selected poems ("Still I Rise," "Phenomenal Woman," or others). Instruct them to read closely to identify themes, literary devices, and powerful imagery.
- Theme Exploration: Divide students into small groups and assign each group a theme prevalent in Angelou's works, such as identity, resilience, social justice, or empowerment. Ask them to analyze how the selected passages and poems exemplify their assigned theme.
- Socratic Seminar: Conduct a Socratic seminar, wherein students discuss their findings from the close reading and theme exploration. Encourage respectful and thoughtful dialogue, allowing students to share their interpretations and engage in meaningful literary analysis.

- Creative Writing: Prompt students to write a reflective essay, poem, or letter to Maya Angelou expressing how her works have impacted them personally and how they see her themes resonate in contemporary society.
- Guest Speaker or Multimedia Resources: Invite a guest speaker, such as a literary scholar or a poet, to share insights into the lasting influence of Maya Angelou's works. Alternatively, show videos of Angelou herself reciting her poetry or delivering speeches.

Assessment Strategies:
- Close Reading Annotations: Assess students' ability to identify literary techniques, themes, and key insights in their close reading annotations.
- Group Presentations: Evaluate each group's presentation on their assigned theme and how Angelou's writings exemplify it.
- Socratic Seminar: Assess students' active participation and contributions to the Socratic seminar discussions.
- Creative Writing: Evaluate students' reflective essays, poems, or letters based on their depth of analysis, clarity of expression, and connection to Maya Angelou's works.

Adapting Content for Diverse Learners:
- Visual Learners: Incorporate visuals, such as photographs and artistic representations of Angelou, to enhance understanding for visual learners.
- Auditory Learners: Use audio clips of Angelou reciting her poetry or delivering speeches to engage auditory learners effectively.
- Kinesthetic Learners: Encourage interactive activities during the Socratic seminar, such as role-playing, to cater to kinesthetic learners' needs.
- English Language Learners (ELL): Provide vocabulary support and offer simplified explanations of complex literary terms when analyzing Angelou's works.

Integration of Prosocial Behaviors:
- Respectful Dialogue: Set clear guidelines for the Socratic seminar to ensure students engage in respectful and inclusive discussions.
- Empathy and Understanding: Encourage students to consider the perspectives of others when analyzing Angelou's themes, fostering empathy and understanding.
- Appreciation and Gratitude: Emphasize the importance of recognizing and appreciating the contributions of influential writers like Maya Angelou, promoting a sense of gratitude for their impact on society.

Note: By immersing themselves in the literary world of Maya Angelou, students will not only explore powerful themes and literary techniques but also recognize the enduring impact of her works on contemporary society. Integrating prosocial behaviors, such as respectful dialogue and empathy, enhances the learning experience and emphasizes the significance of literature as a means of understanding and connecting with the world around us.

The Transformational Education Application Guide *for Groups*

Sections 4D, 4E, 4F, and 4G are designed to serve *groups* for professional development, department collaboration, coaching, mentoring, or faculty- and school-wide initiatives. These sections provide several applications and exercises to help teachers apply the principles of the TE model, which were introduced in the foundational book, *An Introduction to Transformational Education: Redefining Leadership in the Classroom*. These exercises are designed to enhance understanding, promote critical thinking, and provide practical examples for educators. These various applications and exercises in educational theory textbooks aim to bridge the gap between theory and practice, allowing teachers to actively engage with the content and apply it to their teaching contexts.

Section 4D:
Reflection and Discussion

Group discussions promote collaboration and knowledge sharing among teachers. They provide opportunities for educators to discuss and debate educational theories, their applications, and their implications for teaching and learning. This section will explore transformational educators' leadership qualities and practices, focusing on three key aspects: Engagement, Academic Performance, and Prosocial Behaviors.

Instructions: In your group, take turns sharing your thoughts and experiences. Try to keep the discussion focused on the questions provided. Feel free to take notes during your discussion to share your insights with the larger group later.

Group Reflection Questions: Engagement

- Reflect on past experiences in your teaching career when you observed high levels of student engagement in the classroom. What activities or strategies did you implement to foster this engagement, and how did it impact students' overall performance and learning outcomes?
- Remember when you faced challenges in promoting student engagement in your classroom. What obstacles hindered students' involvement in meaningful learning, and how did you address or overcome these challenges? What did you learn from this experience?
- Consider instances when you witnessed transformational school leadership or transformational teacher leadership positively influencing student engagement. How did these leadership styles create an environment that fostered active participation and immersion in learning? What role did you play in supporting or aligning with this type of leadership?
- Based on the text's assertion that engagement is universally viewed as a positive instructional outcome, take a moment to examine your own beliefs and attitudes toward student engagement. How has your understanding of engagement evolved throughout your teaching career, and how has this influenced your instructional practices and approach to student learning?

Group Reflection Questions: Academic Performance
- As an educator, how do you define academic performance, and what measures or criteria do you typically use to assess your students' academic growth and proficiency? How do you ensure that knowledge is retained and the abilities gained are helpful over time?
- Reflecting on existing educational research, how have you observed the relationship between school leadership and student academic achievement in your teaching experience? What evidence or examples support that effective school leadership positively impacts students' academic success?
- The text highlights the significance of teacher behaviors, such as authentic engagement, meaning making, personalized support, and stimulating curiosity, in influencing student achievement. Can you recall instances when you consciously applied these behaviors in your teaching? How did they contribute to your students' academic performance and learning outcomes?
- In your experience as an educator, how have you seen teacher behaviors and the learning climate within your classroom impact student achievement? How do you ensure that your instructional practices align with these factors to create an environment that fosters academic success?

Group Reflection Questions: Prosocial Behaviors
- Looking back on your teaching experiences, can you recall a specific instance where you witnessed the positive impact of prosocial behaviors, such as empathy and kindness, in your classroom or school community? How did these behaviors contribute to creating a strong educational community, and what strategies or approaches did you use to foster these qualities in your students?
- Reflect on the traditional models of teaching and learning that you were exposed to during your education and early teaching career. How did these models address or overlook the importance of prosocial behaviors like empathy and kindness? In what ways do you currently integrate these behaviors into your teaching practices, and how do you see them benefiting your students' overall development?

- As an educator, how do you promote and cultivate prosocial behaviors, such as empathy and kindness, among your students? Have you encountered any challenges in doing so, and if yes, how did you address those challenges? Share some activities or lessons you've implemented to nurture these qualities in your students.
- Based on the observations made by researchers in educational communities aligned with the Transformational Education model, how can you further enhance your role as a teacher in fostering prosocial behaviors? How might authentic engagement, meaning making, personalized support, and stimulating curiosity in your classroom contribute to students demonstrating concern for others, intrinsic motivation to act positively, and acceptance of outgroups?

Section 4E: Peer Mentorship

Having a trusted mentor observe your classroom and offer feedback provides valuable benefits. Their experienced perspective allows for objective observations and constructive criticism, enabling you to gain insights into your teaching practices and areas for improvement. Their guidance helps refine instructional strategies, enhance student engagement, and address specific challenges.

Instructions: Use this one-to-one observation tool with a colleague or mentor to boost your professional growth, expand your teaching repertoire, and foster self-reflection.

Engagement

- The teacher fosters a classroom environment that promotes meaningful learning experiences, encouraging students to be involved and immersed in their work.

Y / N | Comments: _____

_____

- The teacher implements strategies and activities that motivate students to complete homework and actively participate in classroom activities.

Y / N | Comments: _____

_____

- The teacher observes and encourages students to self-monitor their comprehension, helping them articulate their progress in learning and fostering metacognitive skills.

Y / N | Comments: _____

_____

- The teacher maintains a keen awareness of students' attention and participation during classroom activities, ensuring that engagement is observable and encouraged.

Y / N | Comments: _____

_____

- The teacher establishes clear and effective communication with students, providing directions that are readily understood and followed by students.

Y / N | Comments: _____

_____

- The teacher demonstrates Transformational Leadership behaviors, inspiring and motivating students to be engaged in their learning process.

Y / N | Comments: _____

_____

- The teacher utilizes innovative and creative teaching methods to capture students' interest and sustain their engagement throughout lessons.

  Y / N | Comments: _____

- The teacher actively supports and acknowledges students' efforts and accomplishments, reinforcing positive engagement behaviors.

  Y / N | Comments: _____

- The teacher collaborates with other educators and school leadership to create a cohesive approach to promoting student engagement.

  Y / N | Comments: _____

- The teacher continually evaluates and adjusts instructional strategies to enhance student engagement and promote positive instructional outcomes.

  Y / N | Comments: _____

Academic Performance
- The teacher uses various assessment methods, including course grades and standardized tests, to measure and evaluate students' academic performance.

  Y / N | Comments: _____

- The teacher focuses on not only short-term performance but also the durability of learning, ensuring that knowledge is retained and abilities are maintained and useful over time.

  Y / N | Comments: _____

- The teacher is committed to fostering academic quality in students' written work, encouraging them to produce well-structured and well-researched assignments.

  Y / N | Comments: _____

  _____

- The teacher actively engages with students to help them make meaning of the subject matter, ensuring deeper comprehension and understanding.

  Y / N | Comments: _____

  _____

- The teacher provides personalized support to students, addressing individual learning needs and tailoring instruction accordingly.

  Y / N | Comments: _____

  _____

- The teacher creates a learning climate that stimulates curiosity, encouraging students to explore topics further and develop a love for learning.

  Y / N | Comments: _____

  _____

- The teacher demonstrates authentic engagement with students, showing genuine interest and enthusiasm for the subject, which positively impacts student motivation and academic performance.

  Y / N | Comments: _____

  _____

- The teacher's teaching style and behaviors reflect research-backed practices that have been shown to influence student achievement positively.

  Y / N | Comments: _____

  _____

- The teacher fosters a supportive and inclusive classroom environment that encourages students to take risks, ask questions, and actively participate in learning.

Y / N | Comments: _____

_____

- The teacher collaborates with school leadership and other educators to align instructional practices with academic goals, promoting a school-wide culture of academic success.

Y / N | Comments: _____

_____

Prosocial Behaviors
- The teacher demonstrates empathy by actively listening to students' concerns, offering comforting gestures, and providing supportive responses to their emotions.

Y / N | Comments: _____

_____

- The teacher actively promotes and encourages prosocial actions by assigning group projects that require collaboration, facilitating discussions on helping others, and organizing opportunities for students to share resources or assist one another.

Y / N | Comments: _____

_____

- The teacher acts with kindness by using respectful language and tone when addressing students and colleagues, offering assistance willingly, and performing acts of kindness toward students and staff.

Y / N | Comments: _____

_____

- The teacher integrates social and emotional learning activities into the curriculum, such as conducting role-playing exercises to understand different perspectives and discussing scenarios that require empathy and emotional understanding.

Y / N | Comments: _____

_____

- The teacher fosters a sense of community within the classroom by organizing team-building activities, encouraging peer support and cooperation, and addressing conflicts with a focus on understanding and resolving feelings.

Y / N | Comments: _____

_____

- The teacher models prosocial behaviors by openly demonstrating acts of kindness and empathy toward students, colleagues, and visitors to the classroom.

Y / N | Comments: _____

_____

- The teacher provides personalized support to students by offering individualized feedback, taking time to understand students' emotional needs, and tailoring teaching strategies to address students' unique challenges.

Y / N | Comments: _____

_____

- The teacher creates opportunities for meaningful connections among students by facilitating icebreaker activities, group discussions, and collaborative projects that encourage bonding and cooperation.

Y / N | Comments: _____

_____

- The teacher recognizes and reinforces prosocial actions by publicly praising and acknowledging students when they display helpful behaviors, showing appreciation for kindness and empathy in the classroom.

Y / N | Comments: _____

_____

- The teacher encourages acceptance and inclusivity by promoting open discussions on diversity, setting classroom norms that emphasize respect for differences, and intervening when incidents of exclusion or discrimination occur.

Y / N | Comments: _____

_____

Note: Remember that the checklist should be used as a tool to reflect on and improve teaching practices continuously. A teacher's dedication to refining their instructional methods and fostering student engagement is vital in facilitating academic success and overall personal growth in their students.

Section 4F: Scenarios

This section presents a specific teaching scenario and asks teachers to apply the theories and strategies they have learned to address the challenges or opportunities presented. They encourage teachers to think critically, make informed decisions, and consider the practical implications of the theories.

Instructions: Read the following hypothetical scenario that teachers may encounter in their classrooms. Utilize the discussion questions to analyze the situation, identify challenges, and propose solutions based on the theories and concepts discussed in the textbook.

Scenario 1

As the bell rang, signaling the start of the French class at The Lincoln Center, Ms. Haseltine's classroom came alive with energy and excitement. Amy, a bright-eyed and eager student, walked in with a smile, noticing the colorful posters and interactive language games on the walls. Ms. Haseltine greeted each student with genuine warmth, making them feel welcome and valued.

In class, Ms. Haseltine engaged her students through captivating storytelling and role-playing activities. The students became immersed in the French language, laughing and learning together. Amy found herself raising her hand eagerly, wanting to participate in every activity.

Shubh, a shy and reserved student, often sat quietly at the back of the class. Ms. Haseltine noticed his hesitation and approached him with a gentle smile. She spent extra time during breaks, patiently answering his questions and encouraging him to express himself.

As the semester progressed, Ms. Haseltine's teaching style focused on meaningful learning, sparking curiosity in her students. She used real-world examples to explain complex grammar rules and encouraged her students to explore French culture and traditions.

Outside the classroom, Ms. Haseltine organized a community service project. She took her students to a local shelter for immigrants, where they could interact with native French speakers. Amy and Shubh saw firsthand the power of language as a bridge to connect and empathize with others from different backgrounds.

As the semester neared its end, Amy's and Shubh's progress in French was remarkable. They could communicate with confidence and understand the nuances of the language. More importantly, they developed a sense of camaraderie in the class. Whenever someone struggled, others stepped in to offer help and encouragement.

One afternoon, Ms. Haseltine noticed Shubh hesitating while attempting to answer a question. Before she could say anything, Amy, sitting next to him, offered a reassuring smile and whispered a supportive word. Shubh's face brightened, and he answered the question with newfound confidence. It was a small moment but one that spoke volumes about the positive community that had formed in Ms. Haseltine's class.

As the final exams approached, Ms. Haseltine continued to provide personalized support to her students. She recognized their efforts and progress, emphasizing growth and perseverance rather than just grades.

Amy and Shubh, inspired by their teacher's belief in them, pushed themselves to excel.

On the last day of the semester, the class gathered for a farewell party. Ms. Haseltine handed each student a handwritten note, praising their unique strengths and expressing gratitude for their contributions to the class. There were smiles, laughter, and even a few tears as the students realized how much they had grown, not just in their French language skills but also as compassionate individuals.

As Amy and Shubh left the classroom, they shared a newfound appreciation for the transformative power of education. Ms. Haseltine's approach to teaching ignited a passion for learning, fostered empathy, and instilled the value of community mindedness. They knew that the lessons learned in her class would stay with them long after they left the doors of The Lincoln Center, guiding them to live healthy and productive lives filled with kindness and understanding.

Group Discussion:
Using the following, discuss the above scenario considering the student performance principles:

Engagement:
- How did Ms. Haseltine create an engaging learning environment in her French class? What teaching strategies did she use to immerse her students in the language and culture?
- In what ways did Amy demonstrate high levels of engagement in the class? How did her eagerness impact her learning experience?
- Discuss the role of meaningful learning experiences, such as storytelling and role-playing activities, in fostering engagement and enthusiasm among students like Amy and Shubh.

Academic Performance:
- In what ways did Ms. Haseltine's approach to teaching focus on growth and perseverance rather than solely on grades? How did this approach motivate Amy and Shubh to excel academically?
- Discuss the correlation between the students' sense of camaraderie and their academic performance. How might a supportive and compassionate learning environment positively impact students' language learning and academic achievement?

- Reflect on the handwritten notes Ms. Haseltine gave each student on the last day of the semester. How do these personalized acknowledgments of strengths and contributions reinforce the importance of holistic development beyond language skills?

Prosocial Behaviors:
- How did Ms. Haseltine promote prosocial behaviors in her classroom, especially considering Shubh's shyness and reserved nature? How did she encourage empathy and support among the students?
- Analyze the impact of the community service project on Amy, Shubh, and their classmates. How did interacting with native French speakers at the shelter enhance their understanding of empathy and cultural connections?
- Reflect on the small moment when Amy supported Shubh during a challenging moment. How do these instances of kindness and support contribute to the positive community Ms. Haseltine cultivated in her class?

Scenario 2

At Handry High School, Mr. Miller's ninth-grade Intro to Technology class buzzed with excitement as the students gathered around their teacher's desk. Among the bright minds was a pair of twin boys, Shuo and Won, who possessed a deep passion for technology. They dreamed of becoming app developers, hoping to create something that would positively impact people's lives. However, behind their shared enthusiasm lay a layer of shyness that often kept them reserved in the bustling world of the classroom.

Mr. Miller, a patient and empathetic teacher, had a keen eye for recognizing the unique qualities of his students. He noticed the spark of curiosity and talent in Shuo and Won despite their tendency to retreat into the shadows during class discussions. Their quiet nature intrigued him, and he made it his mission to provide them with the support they needed to flourish.

As the semester began, Mr. Miller designed the class in a way that allowed each student to shine, regardless of their level of extroversion. He created a safe and inclusive learning environment where every idea was valued, encouraging even the most introverted students to express themselves. For Shuo and Won, this was a welcome change, as they often found it difficult to voice their thoughts in a room filled with boisterous peers.

During group activities, Mr. Miller carefully paired the twins with classmates who embraced their ideas and encouraged their participation. This strategic approach helped Shuo and Won break out of their shells, as they felt supported and valued by their peers. Slowly but surely, they began to open up, sharing their innovative thoughts with newfound confidence.

Mr. Miller also noticed that Shuo and Won were particularly fascinated by app development. Their eyes would light up whenever he discussed coding and design principles. Recognizing their passion, he offered them additional resources and recommended books and tutorials to hone their skills outside class further.

One day, during a class brainstorming session, Shuo and Won timidly pitched their app idea for "TravelBuddy." Mr. Miller listened attentively, captivated by the brilliance of their vision. He praised their creativity and acknowledged the significance of their dream app, which aimed to revolutionize travel planning for people worldwide.

Seeing the twins' potential, Mr. Miller took it upon himself to be their mentor. He spent one-on-one time with Shuo and Won, discussing their progress and offering guidance. Understanding their shyness, he provided gentle encouragement and ensured they knew their ideas were as valuable as any other student's.

As the weeks passed, Mr. Miller noticed a remarkable transformation in Shuo and Won. Their shyness began to fade, replaced by a newfound self-assurance. They participated actively in class discussions, confidently sharing their perspectives and technical insights. Their peers admired their dedication, and the classroom became a place of support and camaraderie.

With Mr. Miller's guidance, Shuo and Won poured their hearts into creating TravelBuddy. Late nights at the computer turned into moments of joy as the app started taking shape. Mr. Miller offered expert feedback, challenging them to push the boundaries of their coding skills and design aesthetics.

The day of the class presentations finally arrived, and Shuo and Won stood before their peers, nerves mingling with excitement. Mr. Miller stood proudly beside them, offering a reassuring smile. As they showcased TravelBuddy's features and user-friendly interface, their passion shone through. The class was impressed, and the twins' once timid voices rang with conviction and pride.

After the presentation, the classroom erupted into applause, and Shuo and Won received a standing ovation from their peers. Mr. Miller beamed, knowing that this was more than just an app presentation—a celebration of personal growth and overcoming shyness.

As the school year ended, Shuo and Won's bond with Mr. Miller grew stronger. He became more than a teacher; he was a mentor, a guiding light on their path toward achieving their dreams. Their shyness no longer held them back; instead, it became a part of their unique journey to success.

The experience in Mr. Miller's Intro to Technology class at Handry High School became a pivotal moment for Shuo and Won. They realized that their voices mattered and their passion for technology could pave the way for a future they had once thought was beyond their reach. With TravelBuddy as their first step, the twins embarked on a journey that would leave a lasting impact on the world—a testament to the power of a caring teacher and the transformative magic of Handry High School.

Group Discussion:

Using the following, discuss the above scenario considering the student performance principles:

Engagement:
- How did Mr. Miller foster student engagement in his Intro to Technology class, especially for shy students like Shuo and Won?
- What specific teaching strategies did Mr. Miller employ to encourage active participation and meaningful learning in the classroom?
- How did the environment of inclusivity and support contribute to increased engagement among all students, not just Shuo and Won?

Academic Performance:
- Reflecting on Shuo and Won's progress throughout the semester, how did Mr. Miller's approach to academic performance differ from traditional measurement methods (e.g., grades and test scores)?
- How did Mr. Miller's emphasis on personal growth, perseverance, and authentic engagement contribute to the twins' academic success and overall development as learners?
- Discuss the importance of viewing academic performance not solely as knowledge retention but also as the ability to apply skills meaningfully and make a positive impact on the world, as demonstrated by Shuo and Won's app development journey.

Prosocial Behaviors:
- In what ways did Mr. Miller promote prosocial behaviors in his class? How did he encourage empathy, kindness, and collaboration among the students?
- Can you identify any specific instances where the development of prosocial behaviors positively impacted the classroom dynamics or students' interactions with one another?
- How do you think teaching prosocial behaviors alongside academic content can lead to well-rounded, compassionate individuals?

Scenario 3

In the bustling halls of the high school, Mr. Seeford's Intro to Sociology class was about to begin. As the students entered the room, there was an air of indifference among them. Sam and Raul, two unmotivated and underachieving students, reluctantly took their seats at the back of the classroom. They had little interest in the subject and had enrolled in the class only because it was their only option.

Mr. Seeford, a seasoned teacher with a warm smile, sensed the lack of enthusiasm in the room. He knew engaging students like Sam and Raul would be challenging, but he was determined to make a difference in their lives.

Instead of launching into a lecture, Mr. Seeford started the class with an open-ended question. "What do you think sociology is all about?" he asked the students, inviting them to share their thoughts. Sam and Raul exchanged glances, unsure of how to respond. Nevertheless, the question piqued their curiosity, and they listened attentively as their classmates offered their ideas.

Throughout the semester, Mr. Seeford took a hands-on approach to teaching sociology. He organized interactive activities and group discussions, encouraging students to think critically about societal issues and dynamics. Sam and Raul, who had been unenthusiastic at the beginning, found themselves drawn into the discussions as they discovered the relevance of sociology in their daily lives.

One day, Mr. Seeford assigned a project where students had to analyze a social issue that resonated with them. Sam and Raul initially struggled to choose a topic, but with Mr. Seeford's guidance, they settled on examining the impact of community involvement on youth empowerment.

To their surprise, Sam and Raul began to find a sense of purpose in the project. They interviewed local community leaders and their peers, learning about the positive changes that youth activism could bring. Slowly but steadily, they became more engaged in the subject matter, discovering that sociology had the power to uncover meaningful insights about the world around them.

While Mr. Seeford's class was transformative for Sam and Raul, they still occasionally displayed signs of their initial disinterest. They sometimes made offhand remarks during discussions or found small ways to distract their classmates. However, Mr. Seeford never scolded or dismissed them. Instead, he patiently redirected their focus and highlighted their unique perspectives, making them feel valued and respected.

As the semester progressed, Sam and Raul's disruptive behaviors diminished, replaced by a more genuine involvement in class activities. Mr. Seeford noticed the positive changes in their attitudes and praised their efforts, no matter how small they might have seemed.

Toward the end of the semester, Mr. Seeford encouraged the students to reflect on their learning journey. Sam and Raul, in their reflections, expressed gratitude for the unique teaching approach. They acknowledged that they had entered the class with reluctance but had found themselves leaving with a newfound interest and a sense of accomplishment.

In the final weeks, Sam and Raul worked diligently on their project, pouring their hearts into their findings. During the class presentations, they spoke with enthusiasm, sharing their insights and inspiring their peers.

Mr. Seeford's Intro to Sociology class had done wonders for Sam and Raul. They not only improved their academic performance but also developed a newfound appreciation for learning and personal growth. They left the class with greater self-awareness, realizing that even subjects they initially had little interest in could hold valuable life lessons.

As they stepped out of the classroom on the last day of the semester, Sam and Raul thanked Mr. Seeford for being a teacher who saw their potential and believed in their ability to succeed. Mr. Seeford, with a smile of satisfaction, knew that his efforts had made a lasting impact on these two young minds, demonstrating that transformational teaching could ignite a spark of curiosity even in the most unmotivated students.

Group Discussion:
Using the following, discuss the above scenario considering the student performance principles:

1. How did Mr. Seeford's interactive teaching approach in the Intro to Sociology class impact the engagement levels of students like Sam and Raul, who initially had little interest in the subject? Share specific instances from the story that highlight their transformation.

2. Reflecting on the project about community involvement and youth empowerment, how did Sam and Raul's attitudes toward learning change throughout the semester? Discuss the factors contributing to their growing enthusiasm for the subject and its impact on their academic performance.

3. In the story, Mr. Seeford showed patience and understanding when dealing with disruptive behaviors from students like Sam and Raul. How did his approach to classroom management differ from traditional disciplinary methods? How do you think his positive and respectful approach influenced the students' behavior and willingness to participate in class discussions?

Section 4G: Role-Playing

Role-Playing Exercises:

Role-playing activities allow teachers to simulate instructional scenarios or interactions with students. Use the following role-playing exercises to assist you in exploring different teaching approaches, experimenting with strategies, and gaining insights into the practical applications of educational theories.

Role-Play 1

Title: Exploring Holistic Student Performance

Objective: The five-minute role-play displays an interaction between a high school principal and a new student teacher. Ms. Washington, the principal, speaks about student performance to ensure consistency among her staff. Student teacher Sarah welcomes the opportunity to explore these topics.

Roles:
- Ms. Washington: Hilton High School principal
- Sarah Thompson: new student teacher in the History Department

Instructions:

Setting the Scene:
- Principal's office, Hilton High School. Ms. Washington welcomes Sarah into her office.

Role-Play Process:
- Ms. Washington: Good morning, Sarah! I'm glad you could make some time to meet with me. Welcome to Hilton High School. How are you settling in so far?
- Sarah: Good morning, Ms. Washington. Thank you for having me. I'm excited to be here. The staff and students have been very welcoming, and I'm enjoying the experience.
- Ms. Washington: That's wonderful to hear. We're thrilled to have you as part of our team. I wanted to talk to you about the concept of student performance. It's a critical aspect of our educational approach here at Hilton High. Have you had a chance to familiarize yourself with the Transformational Education model we follow?
- Sarah: Yes, I've read about it during my orientation. It emphasizes the importance of transformational teacher behaviors, school climate, and student wellness to improve student performance, not just academically but also in terms of engagement and prosocial behaviors.
- Ms. Washington: Exactly, you've got it. In traditional education, student performance is often measured solely through course grades and standardized test scores. However, we believe in a more holistic view of performance, including academic proficiency, growth, and

- character development. This broader definition considers empathy, kindness, cooperation, and understanding. We call these prosocial behaviors.
- Sarah: That's fascinating, Ms. Washington. Academic performance is crucial, but nurturing empathy and kindness among students seems equally important. It contributes to their overall well-being and success in life.
- Ms. Washington: Precisely. Prosocial behaviors play a significant role in fostering a positive school climate. When teachers model empathy and kindness, students are more likely to respond with the same behaviors, creating a strong educational community. We've seen this happening here at Hilton High School, especially in classrooms where teachers align with the TE model's principles.
- Sarah: I'm impressed with the TE model's focus on engagement as well. It's not just about completing assignments but genuinely immersing students in meaningful learning experiences. I believe that's the key to sparking curiosity and enhancing student performance.
- Ms. Washington: You hit the nail on the head, Sarah. Engaging students is crucial for their progress and success. When students are motivated and actively involved in their learning, they perform better overall. As a new teacher in the History Department, we encourage you to find innovative ways to foster engagement with your students.
- Sarah: I'm eager to do that, Ms. Washington. I can create a stimulating and inclusive learning environment to encourage active participation.
- Ms. Washington: I do not doubt that, Sarah. Your passion for teaching shines through, and I'm confident you'll make a positive impact on your students. Remember, as educators, we play a pivotal role in shaping not only their academic growth but also their development as empathetic and kind individuals.
- Sarah: Thank you for your encouragement, Ms. Washington. I'm excited to be part of a school that values not only academic excellence but also the overall well-being of its students.

- Ms. Washington: You're very welcome, Sarah. If you ever need guidance or support, don't hesitate to reach out. We're here to help you thrive as a teacher and contribute to the success of our students through the principles of Transformational Education.
- Sarah: I truly appreciate that, Ms. Washington. I look forward to learning from experienced educators like you and making a difference in the lives of our students.
- Ms. Washington: I have no doubt you'll do great things here. Welcome aboard, Sarah!

The scene ends with both Ms. Washington and Sarah sharing a smile as they welcome the collaborative journey ahead.

Group Discussion:

After the role-play activity, take some time to reflect as a group on the discussion and consider how you can apply the concepts discussed in your educational context. Think about the crucial role of teacher behaviors in promoting student performance, including engagement, academic performance, and prosocial behaviors. Brainstorm together and explore strategies and interventions that can be implemented to improve the overall performance of your students, such as mentorship programs, creating positive classroom environments, and fostering strong teacher-student relationships. By taking action based on these reflections, you can work toward creating a supportive and transformative educational experience for your students.

1. How does the role-play between Ms. Washington and Sarah in the History Department shed light on the importance of holistic student performance beyond academic achievements? What aspects of the Transformational Education model are applied in their conversation?

2. In the role-play, Ms. Washington emphasizes fostering prosocial behaviors and student engagement. How can teachers effectively incorporate these elements into their teaching practices? Share any ideas or strategies you gathered from the role-play that could be applied in your classroom.

Role-Play 2

Title: The Value and Practice of Prosocial Behaviors

Objective: The five-minute role-play depicts a guidance counselor welcoming a transfer student into her school. The counselor explains the importance of prosocial behaviors to help the student acclimate to his new surroundings.

Roles:
- Ms. Crouse: Mountain View High School guidance counselor
- Lamar: new transfer student-athlete lacrosse player in eleventh grade

Instructions:

Setting the Scene:
- Ms. Crouse's office at Mountain View High School. Ms. Crouse welcomes Lamar with a warm smile.

Role-Play Process:
- Ms. Crouse: Welcome to Mountain View High School, Lamar! I'm Ms. Crouse, the guidance counselor here. I heard you're a new transfer student and also a lacrosse player. It's great to have you here!
- Lamar: (Nervously but politely) Thank you, Ms. Crouse. I'm excited to be here, but I'm also a bit anxious about adjusting to a new school and a new team.
- Ms. Crouse: I understand entirely, Lamar. Moving to a new school can be challenging, but I'm here to help you transition smoothly. We take pride in our school's values and promotion of prosocial behaviors. Have you heard about the Transformational Education model we follow at Mountain View High?
- Lamar: Not really. I've heard about academic performance and stuff, but I'm unsure what prosocial behaviors mean.
- Ms. Crouse: No worries, Lamar. Let me explain. The Transformational Education model goes beyond academic performance. It includes the development of important qualities like empathy and kindness, which we call prosocial behaviors. These behaviors show concern for others, like helping, collaborating, and being respectful and compassionate.
- Lamar: That sounds interesting. Why does the school value these prosocial behaviors?

- Ms. Crouse: Excellent question, Lamar. Promoting prosocial behaviors is crucial because it helps build a positive and supportive school community. When students empathize and show kindness to one another, it creates a strong educational environment where everyone feels valued and accepted. These behaviors are important not just for school but also for life in general. Developing empathy and kindness will help you in your relationships and interactions outside of school as well.
- Lamar: I see how that makes sense. But how do we measure these prosocial behaviors?
- Ms. Crouse: Another good question! While traditional education often focuses solely on academic performance, our TE model recognizes the importance of measuring these nonacademic qualities too. We observe how students engage in meaningful learning, show motivation in completing tasks, and display observable intent to learn. Additionally, we pay attention to actions that demonstrate empathy and kindness, like helping others, collaborating in group work, and showing respect to teachers and peers.
- Lamar: (Nods) That's cool. So, these prosocial behaviors are valued here as much as academic performance?
- Ms. Crouse: Absolutely, Lamar. We believe academic performance and prosocial behaviors are essential for growth and success. Research has shown that students who display prosocial behaviors are more likely to have higher academic performance. It's all interconnected, and we aim to prepare you not only for academic achievements but also to be a caring and responsible community member.
- Lamar: I'm starting to feel more comfortable about being here. It's good to know that the school values more than just grades.
- Ms. Crouse: I'm glad to hear that, Lamar. If you ever need any support, whether it's related to academics, adjusting to the new environment, or anything else, please don't hesitate to reach out to me or any other staff member. We're here to help you thrive academically and personally.
- Lamar: Thank you, Ms. Crouse. I appreciate it.

- Ms. Crouse: You're welcome, Lamar. And remember, as you settle in, don't hesitate to participate in school activities, including sports like lacrosse. It's a great way to build connections and demonstrate those prosocial behaviors we talked about.
- Lamar: I'll keep that in mind. Thanks again.
- Ms. Crouse: You're welcome, Lamar. Have a wonderful time at Mountain View High School, and remember, we're here to support you every step of the way.

Role-play ends with Lamar feeling more at ease and Ms. Crouse being available for ongoing support as he transitions into his new school.

Group Discussions:

1. Reflecting on the role-play interaction between Ms. Crouse and Lamar, how did Ms. Crouse effectively communicate the value and significance of prosocial behaviors in the school's Transformational Education model? How might teachers incorporate similar communication strategies to emphasize the importance of empathy and kindness in their classrooms?

2. In the role-play, Ms. Crouse highlighted the interconnectedness between academic performance and prosocial behaviors. As educators, how can we create learning environments that foster both academic growth and the development of prosocial behaviors? What specific teaching approaches and classroom practices can be implemented to promote empathy, collaboration, and kindness among students?

Section 4H: Interdisciplinary and Collaborative Lesson Planning

The following may be used by school departments, faculty, or for school-wide initiatives. These activities guide teachers in designing lesson plans using the theories and strategies discussed in the textbook. They may involve creating objectives, selecting appropriate instructional methods, developing assessment strategies, and adapting content for diverse learners.

Lesson Plan 1

Title: Interdisciplinary Lesson Planning Activities for Plato's Republic

Grade Level: 9th–12th Grade

Subject Areas: Literature, Philosophy, History, Ethics, and Civics

Lesson Objectives:
- The interdisciplinary lesson planning activities for Plato's Republic aim to provide a comprehensive understanding of the philosophical ideas, historical context, ethical principles, and implications for civic life found in this influential work. By incorporating multiple subject areas, students can explore the text's complexity and relevance to various aspects of human society.

Instructional Methods:
- Lesson 1: Introduction to Plato and Historical Context
- Subject Areas: History, Literature
- Objective: Students will be introduced to the life and times of Plato, understanding the historical context in which he wrote the Republic.
- Activities:
  - Historical Timeline: Students create a timeline of significant events and figures in Ancient Greece during Plato's life.
  - Biographical Research: Groups research and present on key figures of Plato's time, such as Socrates, Aristotle, and other prominent philosophers.
  - Comparing Governments: Students discuss different forms of government prevalent during Plato's era and how they may have influenced his ideas on the ideal state.

- Lesson 2: Philosophical Themes in Plato's Republic
- Subject Areas: Philosophy, Literature
- Objective: Students will explore the philosophical themes and concepts in Plato's Republic.

- Activities:
  - Socratic Dialogues: Divide students into groups and have them perform Socratic dialogues based on key sections of the Republic, exploring themes like justice, the Allegory of the Cave, and the tripartite soul.
  - Philosophical Debate: Organize a class debate on the nature of justice, using arguments from the Republic as reference points.
  - Character Analysis: Students analyze the characters of Socrates, Glaucon, and Thrasymachus, discussing their viewpoints and contributions to the text.
- Lesson 3: Ethical Dilemmas and Virtue in Plato's Republic
- Subject Areas: Ethics, Literature
- Objective: Students will examine the ethical principles and the concept of virtue presented in Plato's Republic.
- Activities:
  - Virtue Ethics Scenario: Students engage in small group discussions, applying the concept of virtue ethics to modern-day scenarios, considering how a virtuous person might act in each situation.
  - The Ring of Gyges: Analyze the story of the Ring of Gyges from the Republic and discuss its implications on human behavior and moral choices.
  - Reflective Journals: Students maintain reflective journals, exploring how the ideas of justice, wisdom, and virtue in the text resonate with their own lives and actions.
- Lesson 4: The Republic and Civic Life
- Subject Areas: Civics, Literature
- Objective: Students will examine the connection between the philosophical ideas in Plato's Republic and their relevance to contemporary civic life.
- Activities:
  - Ideal State Simulation: Organize a simulation activity where students construct their perfect state based on the principles presented in the Republic, discussing how the society would function and its implications.

- Civic Responsibility Discussions: Engage students in discussions on the responsibilities of citizens in a just society and how they can apply these principles to their communities.
- Plato's Influence: Students research and present the influence of Plato's Republic on political thought and governance throughout history.
- By integrating multiple subject areas into the lesson planning activities for Plato's Republic, students can develop a holistic understanding of the philosophical, historical, ethical, and civic aspects of this seminal work. This interdisciplinary approach encourages critical thinking, fosters a deeper appreciation for classical literature, and highlights the enduring relevance of Plato's ideas in shaping human societies.

Lesson Plan 2

Title: Interdisciplinary Lesson Planning Activities for *The Benefits of Being an Octopus* by Ann Braden

Grade Level: 7th Grade

Subject Area: Literature

Lesson Objectives:
- Students will analyze the characters and events in *The Benefits of Being an Octopus* to gain a deeper understanding of empathy, resilience, and social justice.
- Students will explore identity and its impact on an individual's perspective and actions.
- Students will develop critical thinking skills by connecting the book's themes and real-world issues.

Book Overview: *The Benefits of Being an Octopus* is a compelling and thought-provoking novel that delves into the life of seventh-grader Zoey, who deals with poverty, family struggles, and the challenges of navigating middle school. The book addresses empathy, resilience, social justice, and the power of finding one's voice. By integrating various subjects, we can create a comprehensive and enriching learning experience for students while exploring the book's important themes.

Instructional Methods:
- Language Arts: Have students engage in close reading and literary analysis of significant passages in the book. Encourage discussions on character development, emotions, and themes. Use journaling or creative writing exercises to explore characters' perspectives and motivations.
- Social Studies: Investigate the socioeconomic factors and challenges faced by individuals and families living in poverty. Analyze the impact of poverty on access to education, resources, and opportunities. Discuss historical and contemporary social justice movements.
- Science: Discuss animal behaviors, focusing on octopuses and their adaptations. Relate the octopus's ability to adapt to the story's theme of resilience. Explore ecological concepts, such as the

interconnectedness of ecosystems, linking them to the characters' experiences.
- Mathematics: Create real-life scenarios related to budgeting and financial planning to understand Zoey's family struggles. Calculate and analyze data on poverty rates and income disparities in the community or country, highlighting the importance of social justice.
- Art: Encourage students to create visual representations, such as illustrations, collages, or posters, depicting the book's themes and messages. Use art as a medium for students to express their experiences and perspectives on empathy and resilience.
- Drama: Organize a role-play or skit where students reenact significant scenes from the book, exploring different characters' viewpoints and emotions. This activity will enhance students' understanding of empathy and identity.

Assessment Strategies:
- Literature Analysis: Evaluate students' close reading annotations and class discussions to assess their comprehension of the book's themes and characters.
- Interdisciplinary Projects: Review students' projects, creative writing, and artwork to gauge their ability to connect the book's themes to various subjects.
- Group Presentations: Assess students' presentations on social justice issues, including their ability to analyze data and connect to the book's narrative.
- Empathy Journal: Have students keep an empathy journal throughout the reading, where they reflect on the characters' emotions and experiences, leading to discussions on empathy and understanding.

Adapting Content for Diverse Learners:
- Visual Learners: Incorporate visuals, such as illustrations or diagrams, to aid visual learners' understanding of complex concepts and themes.
- Auditory Learners: Use read-aloud sessions or audiobooks for auditory learners to engage with the content effectively.

- Kinesthetic Learners: Include hands-on activities, such as role-playing and interactive projects, to cater to kinesthetic learners' needs.
- English Language Learners (ELL): Provide vocabulary support, use simplified language, and offer additional resources to accommodate ELL students' needs.

Integration of Prosocial Behaviors:
- Classroom Norms: Establish a positive and inclusive classroom environment where empathy, respect, and understanding are encouraged and valued.
- Cooperative Learning: Promote teamwork and collaboration during interdisciplinary activities, fostering prosocial behaviors and mutual support.
- Empathy Practice: Engage students in discussions and activities that help develop their empathy toward characters in the book and real-world issues.

By creating an interdisciplinary lesson plan for *The Benefits of Being an Octopus*, teachers can offer a holistic and meaningful learning experience for seventh-grade students. Through close reading, thematic exploration, and hands-on projects, students will develop critical thinking skills and empathy, enabling them to connect literature and the real world. Integrating prosocial behaviors fosters a positive learning environment, promoting character development and social awareness among students.

Lesson Plan 3

Title: World Language Department Wide Plan: Exploring *Cien años de Soledad* (*One Hundred Years of Solitude*) by Gabriel García Márquez

Grade Level: 12th Grade

Subject Area: Literature

Lesson Objectives:
The objective of this department-wide plan is to facilitate a comprehensive and engaging exploration of Gabriel García Márquez's novel *Cien años de Soledad* (*One Hundred Years of Solitude*) across various world language courses. The plan aims to enable teachers to design lesson plans that incorporate different instructional methods, promote critical thinking and literary analysis, and adapt content to meet the needs of diverse learners.

Instructional Methods and Activities:

Prereading Activities:
- Conduct a multimedia presentation on Gabriel García Márquez, the historical context, and the literary significance of the novel.
- Engage students in a discussion on the themes and cultural aspects of the book to build anticipation and curiosity.

Close Reading and Literary Analysis:
- Facilitate guided reading sessions with selected passages to promote a deeper understanding of the author's style, language, and symbolism.
- Utilize Socratic seminars or group discussions to encourage critical thinking and analysis of complex themes within the novel.

Character Analysis and Role-Playing:
- Assign students specific characters from the book and have them present their interpretations through role-playing or monologues.
- Encourage students to explore the characters' motivations and actions to gain insight into the novel's complexities.

Creative Writing and Response Journals:
- Promote creativity and self-expression by assigning students to write alternate endings, additional chapters, or personal reflections in response to the novel.
- Implement response journals to encourage students to share their thoughts, questions, and connections to the text throughout their reading journey.

Visual Representations:
- Organize an art project where students create visual representations of key scenes or themes from the novel using various art mediums.
- Host a book cover design competition to encourage students' artistic expression and interpretation of the story.

Cultural Connections:
- Invite guest speakers or conduct virtual meetings with individuals from Colombian or Latin American cultural backgrounds to discuss the novel's cultural relevance.
- Organize a cultural fair where students present aspects of Colombian culture portrayed in the novel, such as traditional music, food, and customs.

Assessment Strategies:

Reading Quizzes and Annotations:
- Administer reading quizzes to assess students' comprehension and progress throughout the novel.
- Evaluate students' close reading annotations to gauge their engagement and understanding.

Literary Analysis Essays:
- Assign essays that require students to analyze specific themes, symbols, or literary devices present in *Cien años de Soledad*.
- Provide rubrics to assess the depth of their analysis, organization, and writing skills.

Presentations and Performances:
- Evaluate students' character role-playing or monologues based on their interpretation and understanding of the characters.
- Assess group presentations on cultural aspects or visual representations based on creativity, clarity, and cultural accuracy.

Adapting Content for Diverse Learners:

Multimodal Resources:
- Provide audiobooks or audio summaries for students who may benefit from auditory learning.
- Incorporate visuals and graphics to support visual learners in understanding complex concepts.

Scaffolded Activities:
- Offer differentiated reading materials or abridged versions of the novel for students who require additional support.
- Provide sentence starters or graphic organizers to assist students in organizing their ideas during writing tasks.

Collaborative Learning:
- Encourage peer collaboration during group discussions and presentations, allowing students to learn from one another and share diverse perspectives.

Culturally Responsive Teaching:
- Incorporate culturally relevant materials and texts from various Latin American authors to cater to diverse cultural backgrounds in the classroom.

By implementing this department-wide plan, teachers can foster a deep appreciation for Gabriel García Márquez's literary masterpiece *Cien años de Soledad* in their world language classes. By incorporating diverse instructional methods and assessment strategies and adapting content for diverse learners, students will engage with the novel's themes, cultural significance, and linguistic richness. Through critical thinking and creative exploration, students will gain a deeper understanding of Latin American literature and its impact on global literature and culture.

Lesson Plan 4

Title: High School History Department-Wide Plan: Exploring the Work of 2022 Peace Prize Awardee Ales Bialiatski

Grade Level: 9th–12th Grade

Subject Area: History

Lesson Objectives:
The objective of this department-wide plan is to introduce students to the work and contributions of Ales Bialiatski, the 2022 Peace Prize awardee from Belarus. By engaging students in meaningful historical exploration, we aim to foster critical thinking, empathy, and understanding of human rights advocacy and its significance in shaping contemporary global issues.

Instructional Methods:
- Biography and Historical Context: Start the lesson by providing students with background information on Ales Bialiatski's life and the sociopolitical context of Belarus. Use multimedia resources, documentaries, and primary sources to enhance understanding.
- Research and Analysis: Assign students to research Ales Bialiatski's activism and human rights advocacy. They can explore his contributions to democracy, civil rights, and the challenges faced in Belarus.
- Panel Discussion: Organize a panel discussion with guest speakers knowledgeable about human rights issues, democracy, and activism in Belarus. Encourage students to prepare questions for the panelists.
- Interactive Timeline: Ask students to create an interactive timeline of significant events in Ales Bialiatski's life and the human rights movements in Belarus. This can be done using digital tools or posters.
- Role-Playing Activity: Divide students into small groups and have them role-play scenarios where they advocate for human rights in a challenging environment, drawing inspiration from Ales Bialiatski's experiences.

- Global Connections: Encourage students to analyze how Ales Bialiatski's work connects to other global human rights movements, such as the struggle for democracy in other countries.
- Creative Expression: Allow students to express their understanding of Ales Bialiatski's work through creative projects, such as art, poetry, or short films.

Assessment Strategies:
- Research Presentation: Assess students' research presentations on Ales Bialiatski's life, contributions, and the challenges faced in his advocacy work.
- Panel Discussion Participation: Evaluate students' engagement and critical thinking during the panel discussion.
- Interactive Timeline: Assess the accuracy and depth of students' interactive timelines and their ability to contextualize events.
- Role-Playing Activity: Evaluate students' understanding of human rights issues and their ability to apply advocacy skills in challenging scenarios.
- Global Connections Essay: Assess students' essays discussing the connections between Ales Bialiatski's work and other global human rights movements.
- Creative Expression: Evaluate students' creative projects, assessing how well they capture the essence of Ales Bialiatski's activism.

Adapting Content for Diverse Learners:
- Visual Learners: Use visual aids, such as infographics and videos, to support the understanding of historical context and Ales Bialiatski's work.
- Auditory Learners: Include audio clips or podcasts related to human rights activism in Belarus to engage auditory learners.
- Kinesthetic Learners: Incorporate hands-on activities, like the role-playing scenario, to cater to kinesthetic learners' needs.
- English Language Learners (ELL): Provide vocabulary support, simplified language, and bilingual resources to accommodate ELL students in understanding the historical context and complex human rights concepts.

Integration of Prosocial Behaviors:
- Respectful Dialogue: Foster an environment of respectful dialogue during the panel discussion, encouraging students to listen and empathize with different perspectives.
- Empathy and Understanding: Emphasize the importance of understanding the challenges faced by activists like Ales Bialiatski and the people of Belarus.
- Advocacy for Change: Encourage students to explore ways to advocate and support human rights causes in their communities.

By implementing this department-wide plan, history teachers can offer students a comprehensive and empathetic understanding of Ales Bialiatski's work and its broader implications for human rights advocacy. By encouraging critical thinking, creative expression, and respectful dialogue, students will be equipped to engage thoughtfully with complex historical and contemporary global issues. The integration of prosocial behaviors ensures that students develop not only historical knowledge but also a sense of empathy and agency in shaping a just and equitable world.

www.ingramcontent.com/pod-product-compliance
Lightning Source LLC
Chambersburg PA
CBHW081354290426
44110CB00018B/2370